Andrew Summers Rowan, Marathon Montrose Ramsey

The Island of Cuba

Andrew Summers Rowan, Marathon Montrose Ramsey

The Island of Cuba

ISBN/EAN: 9783337379261

Printed in Europe, USA, Canada, Australia, Japan

Cover: Foto ©ninafisch / pixelio.de

More available books at **www.hansebooks.com**

THE ISLAND OF CUBA

A DESCRIPTIVE AND HISTORICAL ACCOUNT OF THE "GREAT ANTILLA"

"La mas fermosa tierra que jamas ojos vieron."
—CRISTÓBAL COLÓN

BY

ANDREW SUMMERS ROWAN

First Lieutenant, 19th Infantry, U. S. Army. Sometime Member of the Intercontinental Railway Survey

AND

MARATHON MONTROSE RAMSEY, B. S., A. M.

Professor of Romance Languages in the Columbian University. Author of "A Text-Book of Modern Spanish"

NEW YORK

HENRY HOLT AND COMPANY

1896

los Colorados
Guadiyumairo
PINAR
Pinar del Río
ISLA DE PINOS
CANAL VIEJO
Pto. PPE.
MAR DE

PREFACE.

It is a phase of the law of supply and demand that, whenever any unfamiliar topic, place, or person begins to assume prominence before the public, the very demand for information which its importance brings about will produce a supply of literature bearing upon it.

Such has been the case with Cuba. During the first half of the present century people outside its own shores, to use a familiar expression, " knew little and cared less " about it. The public attention which was attracted by the rebellion of 1868 was answered by numerous descriptive and historical works; and its political rights and wrongs were commented upon in numerous treatises, impartial or polemic. But when, after the capitulation at El Zanjón, ten years later, the contending factions on the island ceased to support their respective views by force of arms, the outside world heard less and less of Cuba and her affairs, until they became no longer a matter of public interest.

Indeed, so little have we been concerned with the island—which, on account of its proximity to our shores, if for no other reason, should have some claim to our consideration—that, according to the results of a search instituted in the Copyright Office of the Library of Congress, but six works upon Cuba were published in this country between the years of 1870 and 1889, and only one during the years from 1890 to 1895; while a file of the annual "English Catalogue of Books" from 1885 to 1895 does not contain the title of a single such work printed in Great Britain and Ireland.

We might naturally expect that the attention again centered upon the Island of Cuba by the recurrence of hostilities in 1895 would be promptly followed by a new output of literature; and this has proved to be the case. Three works of some magnitude have already appeared in the United States this year, besides a flood of small pamphlets and articles.

It might seem, therefore, that to add another book upon the subject would be both uncalled for and unnecessary. But when we find, upon examination, how very little has been said or written that has been unbiased by personal preference or partisan feeling, and how great a proportion of this new growth of literature is of an ephemeral and even of a superficial character, there may yet appear to be room for a work such as is now laid before the public.

The tendency of modern writings, so far as they are not merely ornamental or fanciful, is largely scientific. Science is but another name for system. Our modern requirements now insist that the writer of— for example — a history, shall make no assertion that he has not substantiated, either by reference to the writings of a recognized authority, or by the examination of original records, or by his own personal experience; that he shall arrange his material logically; and shall strive to give, so far as possible, cause and effect. These requirements have further resulted in the tendency to employ specialists, and to assign the various branches of a subject to persons best qualified to treat them.

The writers of the following pages had occasion recently, in connection with the discharge of official duties, to make some investigations relative to Cuba and its relations to the United States. It then occurred to them that some part of the facts thus brought to their knowledge might be of interest to the public. In the arrangement of the work to be undertaken, the previous lines of investigation of the respective collaborators were kept in view, and the book was divided accordingly. The first part contains a detailed description of the physical conditions of the island; the second or historical part narrates what has been done on this scene of action; the third part describes the present condition of the island from an administrative and commercial standpoint. As the primary object of the authors was to gain correct information and not to dress up a tale of woe or defend a party, they have endeavored to divest themselves of passion and prejudice, and to present the truth as nearly as they could find it.

The Cuban question is not an easy or simple one. There are at least four points of view, and perhaps we should rather say five.

To those who look from only one of these, the affair is very simple.

1. The Cubans find themselves heavily taxed under an ever-changing government of Europeans, upon which they have no effective influence.

2. Spain, on the verge of utter bankruptcy, cannot afford to lose money or spend money on Cuba, and yet is compelled to do both in order to maintain her dominion over the island.

3. The holders of Spanish securities may be often religious, educational, or charitable institutions, or widows and orphans, whose scanty means have been invested in that precarious lottery.

4. England and France are appealed to by the bondholders for protection, and are unwilling to see Cuba pass into the possession of anyone strong enough to make any real use of it.

5. The government of the United States has all this and a great deal more as a problem to figure out.

M. M. R.

COLUMBIAN UNIVERSITY,
WASHINGTON, *May*, 1896.

CONTENTS.

PART III.

POLITICAL AND COMMERCIAL.

THE ISLAND OF CUBA

PART I.

DESCRIPTIVE.

By Lieut. A. S. Rowan, U. S. Army.

POSITION AND EXTENT.

The Island of Cuba lies just within the north torrid zone, immediately south of the State of Florida. The meridian of Washington crosses it at its widest part, about 250 miles east of Habana and about 200 miles west of Cape Maisí, the most eastern point.

The distance from the northwest coast of Cuba to the Florida mainland is only about that which separates New York from Albany, or Washington from Philadelphia on the one hand and Norfolk on the other.*

The length of the island, measured on its median line from Cape Maisí to Cape San Antonio (11 degrees of longitude in the latitude of 20° N. to 23° N.), is about 760 miles; and the breadth, measured at the narrowest part, which is in the vicinity of Habana, is from 30 to 36 miles. The widest part is in the east, where, measured on the meridian of Mazanillo at the mouth of the Río Cauto, the breadth is 125 miles.

If the island of Cuba were translated to the latitude of New York, and Cape Maisí were

* The following distances may be useful for reference :

Key West to nearest point on the Cuban coast,	86 miles.
Key West to Habana, ...	93 "
New York to Habana, ...	1413 "
New Orleans to Habana, ...	475 "
Cape San Antonio, Cuba, to Cape Catoche, Yucatán, ...	125 "
Santiago de Cuba to Kingston, Jamaica, . .	200 "
Santiago de Cuba to Greytown (entrance to Nicaragua Canal), ...	700 "

laid down at Sandy Hook, Cape San Antonio would occupy a position in the vicinity of Chicago. In other words, one of the New York Central's fastest trains would require nearly twenty-four hours to pass from one end of the island to the other; while to cross it in the vicinity of Habana would be approximate in time to a trip from Washington to Baltimore, or, if crossed in the vicinity of Santiago, to a trip from New York City to Albany.

The form of the island * is that of a thin, irregular crescent with the convex side on the north, nearly tangent to the Tropic of Cancer. It has a coast line of about 2200 miles (according to Pichardo), or, if we include all indentations, nearly 7000 miles. About half of the north coast is open, as is also an equal proportion of the south coast, offering many fine harbors, generally with narrow entrances, and capable of easy defense. The remainder is screened by a multitude of small islands (grouped in four archipelagoes), keys, and banks, which render navigation difficult, dangerous, and in many parts impracticable.

* Humboldt likens Cuba to Java, in shape, size, products, and position.

While this long and narrow figure of the island permits of ready water communication, it has to some extent retarded the development of its resources by not demanding the construction of railways.

The area of Cuba is about 45,000 square miles—being one-fourth that of Spain, or approximately equal to the State of Pennsylvania.

The favorable position of the island, lying at the mouth of the Gulf of Mexico, and so near the three great divisions of the western hemisphere, has caused Habana, its capital, to be called the " Key to the New World."

TERRITORIAL DIVISIONS.

Popularly the island is divided into four regions known respectively as the Vuelta Abajo (the lower turn), Vuelta Arriba (the upper turn), Las Cinco Villas (the five towns), and the Tierra Adentro (the interior country).

From the meridian of Habana to Cape San Antonio lies the Vuelta Abajo. This is again popularly subdivided by giving the name of los Partidos de fuera (the outlying portions), or simply los Partidos, to the

CANAL DE S.N
Bajos de los Colorados
Guaniguanico
Pinar del Río
ISLA DE PINOS
Ciénaga de Zapata
Colón
Macagua y Palmillas
Sta. Isabel de Las Lajas
Cienfuegos
Sierra de San y Trinidad
Trinidad

part between the meridian of Habana and that of San Cristóbal in Pinar del Río.

From the meridian of Habana eastward to that of Santa Clara lies the Vuelta Arriba.

From the meridian of Santa Clara to that of Puerto Príncipe, or even as far east as Holguín, the term Las Cinco Villas is now applied (formerly called Las Cuatro Villas, the four towns, from the four towns of Trinidad, Remedios, Santo Espíritu, and Santa Clara). The new designation is taken from the jurisdictions of Sagua, Santa Clara, Trinidad, Remedios, and Cienfuegos; but the original five " towns " have since been elevated to the rank of " cities."

The Tierra Adentro (the interior) may be roughly defined as lying between the meridian of Caibarién and the extreme eastern point of the island.

It will be seen that there is frequently an overlap in the limits of these popular divisions, but this is of no definite importance. It is extremely convenient, however, to be familiar with these designations, as they are referred to constantly in writings and in conversation.

In its ecclesiastical concept, the island is

divided into two dioceses, viz.: the arch-bishopric of Santiago de Cuba, and the bishopric of Habana—the divisional line separating the island into two equal portions.

Politically there are six provinces (see Map No. 1), which take the names of their respective capital cities. Beginning at the west they are: Pinar del Río, Habana, Matanzas, Santa Clara, Puerto Príncipe, and Santiago de Cuba. These are again subdivided into judicial districts and municipalities.

OROGRAPHY.

Although Cuba is known as a mountainous country, its orographical features are not, in all parts, well defined. In a general way a mountain chain may be said to extend from Cape Cruz, passing close to the seacoast, eastward to Cape Maisí. Then, turning abruptly to the west, it passes along the middle of the island, breaking away here and there, first to the north coast, then to the south, and then following a central line till it fades away in the marshes of Cape San Antonio. The symmetrical position of the culminating ridge causes a nearly equal distribution of the number of streams and the volumes of water

carried to the north and south of the cordillera.

The main chain or sierra, approximating in
length to 1000 miles, is broken into groups
bearing distinctive names and separated by
rolling uplands, or by low-lying plains elevated only a few hundred feet above the sea.

In the province of Santiago de Cuba the
range extending from Cape Cruz along the
southern coast toward Cape Maisí forms a
junction in the central and eastern parts with
that traversing the middle of the island, cre-
ating, as might be anticipated, an intricate
system of verdure-clad elevations cut into
sharp and well-defined ridges known as cuchillas, or " knife-edged " crests, as distinguished from the series of peaks generally
styled sierras or " saws." The first mentioned range is called the Sierra Maestra or
" Master " range and is the best defined
mountain chain on the island. From Cape
Cruz it rises first in a succession of terraces,
and soon attains the altitude of 5140 feet at
the crest of the Ojo del Toro (bull's eye)
peak, 20 miles from the cape. This increase
in elevation is continued as the crest of the
sierra is followed eastward until it culminates,

at a height of 8320 feet, or more, in the celebrated Blue Peak or Pico Turquino (sometimes erroneously written " Tarquino ") about halfway between Cape Cruz and Santiago de Cuba. Near the Turquino, spurs are sent off toward the north into the valley of the Cauto as far as the vicinity of Bayamo, giving an undulating character to the south side of that famous tropical valley. From the Turquino eastward the name of Sierra Maestra is dropped and that of Sierra de Cobre, or " copper range," is substituted. Here are found the copper mines of Santiago de Cuba.

In the Cobre range, a short distance east of Santiago de Cuba, is a great block of conglomerate, measuring 150 feet in length by 45 feet in width, resting on the top of a truncated pyramidal peak 3300 feet above the sea and known as La Gran Piedra. In this vicinity the southern coast range, the Sierra Maestra proper, is merged with the main backbone of the island coming from Cape San Antonio on the west, and the maze of the Cuchillas becomes now the dominating orographical feature; while a great number of streams rising close together send their waters into far separated seas. This extremely broken and precipitous country, occupying as it does a large part of an entire province, has caused it to be the least known, as it is the most difficult of access, of any of the political divisions of the island. Roads here are few and poor; but the great diversity of products, due to the rapid change in the climate which is caused by the difference in elevation, makes this region one of the most wonderful in the world. The cascades, cataracts, and natural portals, surrounded by an ever verdant foliage, combined with numerous species of flowering orchids and other tropical flowers, and with animal life in all its gayest colors, present a picture such as is furnished at but few points on the globe. Well might Columbus write to his sovereign that here was to be found "the fairest land that the sun shines on or that the eye has ever seen."

Turning now westward and following the crest of the central chain, a very notable truncated cone over 3000 feet high is to be seen near the port of Baracoa. This remarkable peak, long known to navigators, bears the name El Yunque de Baracoa, (the anvil of Baracoa).

Near the meridian of Nipe the decrease in elevation is quite marked and the mountains begin to dip into the plain until, between the Bay of Nuevitas and the inlet of Esperanza, they are no longer perceptible. Only here and there detached groups appear, as in the Sierra de Guaycanamar, south of Puerto Príncipe, and in the Sierra de Cubitas, immediately to the north of that city. The Cubitas range, always noted for its great caves, has recently come into historical prominence by reason of its selection as the seat of the new insurgent government.

Still moving toward the west over the undulating, forest-clad plains, the next group of mountains observed is that of the Sierra de Bamburanao, a local range subdivided into four groups, the whole reaching as far as San Juan de los Remedios and terminating there in the marshes on the north coast.

In passing from the Cubitas group to that of Bamburanao, the island, now less than 50 miles wide, is little above the level of the sea; and across this low, narrow reach the military line of La Trocha (or " the trench "), with detached forts at short intervals, was established during the insurrection of 1868-

FIRST TROCHA.
Scale of Miles.
0 5 10 20 30
22° 40
CAYO FRANCES
CAYO DE S. MARIA
CAYO MEDIA LUNA
CAYO COCO
Bahía de Buenavista
LA GAGUA
DE TIRIGUANO
Boca de la Yana
Mayajigua
Matahambre
Jatibonico del Norte
El Calnagueyano
Ranchuelo
Morón
Mt. Cunagua
Guadalupe
Concepción
Caño de la Yana
Adivisoria
Ciego de Avila
Jucibonico del Sur
S. Ant° Abaô del Jibaro
Malarrecua
Jucaro
S. Geronimo
CAYOS ANA MARIA
21° 20
79°
West of Greenwich
78° 20'

78 to confine the operations of the insurgents
to the eastern departments. (See sketch.)
This line passes approximately north and
south through Morón and Ciego de Avila, and
has its flanks resting in the tangled mangrove
swamps of the coasts.

A little further westward, but over against
the southern shore, leaving a longitudinal
valley (through which the railway line from
Habana or Pinar del Río will pass on its way
to Santiago de Cuba), is the Sierra de San
Juan y Trinidad. "This calcareous group,"
says Humboldt, "has a majestic aspect as seen
near the Cayo de Piedras. . . The land
in the interior of the island is gently undu-
lated as in England." The dominating peak
of the central or Santa Clara mountain region
is in this southern (San Juan) group, near
the sea, not far from the town of Trinidad,
and bears the name of El Pico del Potrillo.
It has an altitude of about 3000 feet. The
range from this point passes slightly to the
northwest and then curves around to the
south, forming the background to the land-
locked bay of Cienfuegos, the ancient
Xagua. Projecting westward from the ter-
minal point is the celebrated Ciénaga de

Zapata or " shoe-shaped " marsh, which juts out into the sea, forming on its north the Ensenada (inlet) de la Broa.

Another depression of the rolling upland occurs between the San Juan range and the highlands on the north coast skirting the Matanzas bay—the highest point (1300 feet) of the latter being the great Pan de Matanzas (Matanzas loaf), so named from its resemblance to a loaf of sugar. The Pan has had great celebrity among navigators, as from it they have long been accustomed to get their bearings off a dangerous coast none too well marked by artificial aids to navigation.

Westward from Matanzas the dividing ridge, locally known as the Cordillera de los Organos, is more continuous, following the crescent line of the north shore until it culminates in the Pan de Guajaibón, a peak 2000 feet in height. Thence westward the elevation gradually declines and broadens out till it reaches the terminating peak, the Cerro de la Cabra, which is west of Pinar del Río. Then comes a rapid descent, and the last disjointed vertebra of the island disappears in the sandy dunes and low-lying marshes of Cape San Antonio, which mark this end of Cuba in striking contrast to the towering elevations of Cape Maisí at the east.*

To recapitulate, it may be stated in general terms that the island possesses a central mountain chain reaching from Guardiana Bay to Cape Maisí and then bending around to the south and west to Cape Cruz—attaining, in places, great elevation, and again almost dropping to the sea level. In all the aggregation of mountains there is but one well-defined, continuous chain—the Sierra Maestra. Finally, the island may be conveniently considered as divided into three orographic districts or groups, designated respectively as the Western or Pinar del Río group, the Central or Santa Clara and Matanzas groups, and the Eastern or Santiago group.

The western district, extending from Cape San Antonio to the meridian of Point Hicacos, includes the narrowest part of the island, and is very mountainous and broken. The northern slopes are watered by many small

---

* The decreasing level of the limestone formations of the island of Cuba toward the north and west indicates the submarine connection of those rocks with the lands equally low of . . . Florida.—*Humboldt.*

streams. The slope to the south coast is gradual; in the interior the country is fertile, but is very marshy near the coast. Here, between the Bay of Cortés on the west and the village of Majana on the east, are the vast tobacco plantations that have made the Vuelta Abajo rich and famous. From Majana eastward to the Maribeque River is the zoophitic district, in which are found the great caves of Gabriel, Turibacoa, Jaiguán, Guanimar, and many others.

The central zone may be defined as lying between Matanzas and the western boundary of the province of Puerto Príncipe. It contains the best and also the worst land on the island, for by the side of the extremely fertile plains, watered by many rivers, are to be found districts entirely sterile. The north and south coasts, covered by a skirmish line of reefs and keys, are low and marshy except for a few stretches of limited extent.

In the eastern zone, the districts to the north and south of Puerto Príncipe are quite low and flat, except in the sporadic mountain clusters previously alluded to. The plains of the north coast are marshy, but as we penetrate inland we find them becoming sandy and barren. The southern plains of this zone, although sometimes overflowed along the coast, are in the interior covered with fine pastures and luxuriant forests. The eastern extremity is, as already stated, very mountainous, cut up with copious streams, and interspersed with tracts of great fertility.

There are no active volcanoes on the island, but many extinct ones are recognizable in the characteristic cones, and in the pumice and other plutonic rocks of which they are composed. It is quite evident that the Ojo del Toro, Pico Turquino, and others were formerly active.

Earthquakes occur chiefly in the province of Santiago de Cuba. That of 1776, when our forefathers were beginning their struggle for independence, was remarkable for its severity and the ruin it wrought, as was that of 1842, and, above all, that of 1852. Elsewhere in the island these convulsions have been rare and much less destructive.

WATER COURSES.

From the shape and formation of Cuba, and from its orographical features, it is obvious that the rivers, while they may be great in number, cannot be so in length.* Yet from the large amount of rainfall in the wet season, the streams at that time carry great volumes of water.

The Cuban mountains, formed of metamorphic rocks, appear to have had deposited upon them a thick layer of calcareous material, reaching down the slopes to the coast marshes; and it is only in some places that the underlying older formations project, like the vertebræ of some gigantic extinct animal, half buried in the seas and its own detritus—the limestone formation representing the ancient flesh, the vegetable mold the cuticle, and the vegetation the hairy covering.

And more, this carcass is nearly all hollow within, for the descending water has dissolved the limestone, forming long underground galleries into which it plunges to appear and disappear again, or to lie in great cavernous

* The cavernous texture of the limestone formations, the great inclination of their shelves, the smallness [narrowness] of the island, the frequency and nakedness of the plains . . . may be considered among the principal causes of the want of rivers and the drought which is felt, especially in the western part of Cuba.—*Humboldt.*

reservoirs, from which, on account of their elevation, it is often forced by hydrostatic pressure fresh to the surface far out at sea. Elisée Réclus tells us that "in the Jardines [east of the Isle of Pinos], so named from the verdure-clad islets strewn like gardens amid the blue waters, springs of fresh water bubble up from the deep, flowing probably in subterranean galleries from the mainland."

There are few countries in the world more remarkable for the size and number of their subterranean cavities than this long and narrow "Pearl of the Antilles." Among the most remarkable and famous caves are those of Resolladero Guacanaya, in Guaniguanico; María Belén, in the Sierra de Añafe; that of Cotilla, near San José de las Lajas, fifteen miles southeast of Habana; the magnificent caves of Bellamar in Matanzas; and those of San José de los Remedios; together with the caverns of Cubitas, of Gibara, of Yumurí, of Holguín, and of Bayamo, while north of Guantánamo are the noted Monte Líbano caverns.

Among the streams that "lose themselves" is the Río San Antonio, in the province of Habana, which drains the wonderful

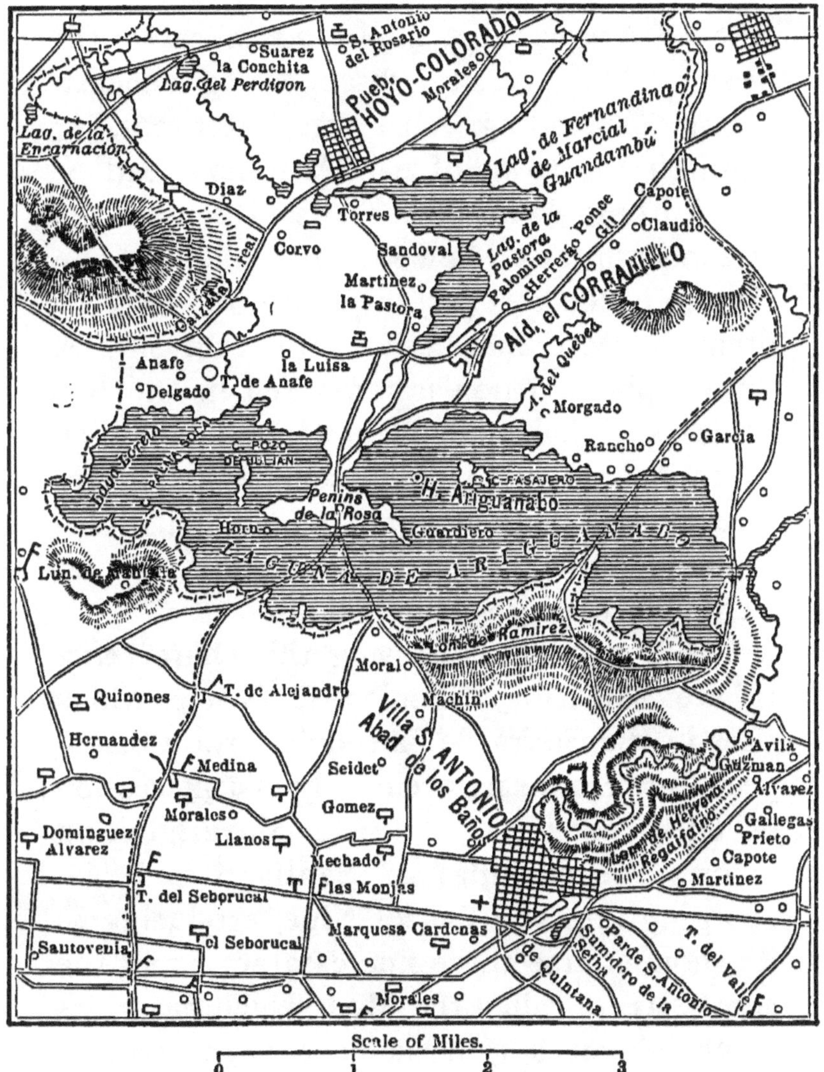

Scale of Miles.

0   1   2   3

lake of Ariguanabo, about 20 miles south-west of Habana city, disappearing beneath a large, spreading ceiba tree, after passing through the town of San Antonio Abad or San Antonio de los Baños. On the maps the streams appear to flow into the lake; but the reverse is the case, as, in reality, it serves to drain the latter and keep its waters fresh. A similar phenomenon is remarked in the Río de las Capellanías or Río Guanajay, which takes its rise in the Mesa del Mariel, flows directly south for a dozen miles, and disappears near the village of San Andrés, not far from the railway station.

Other streams possessing this characteristic are: the Río Jatibonico del Norte, which rises in the Sierra de Jatibonico, soon disappears, and reappears eventually in a succession of noisy cascades; the Río Mayari, rising among the cuchillas of Santiago and discharging into the Bay of Nipe, producing in its short course three fine cataracts; and the short stream called the Moa, which has in its chief affluent a remarkable cataract with a fall of 300 feet, and also a cave into which it plunges to appear again further down. The latter, like the Río Mayari, is born among the cuchillas, and flows into the sea on the north coast.

The Macaguanigua, which empties into the Baracoa bay, besides having had " pearls in its mouth," has also in its affluent, the Minas, a most beautiful cascade.

The San Diego, taking its rise in the high and thin ridges of the Gavilanes (province of Pinar del Río), passes in its course under some beautiful natural arches or bridges called Los Portales.

So much for the wonderful cataracts and caves of Cuba, a study and a marvel in themselves, but which here can only be referred to, not described.

As before stated, the rivers of Cuba are many, rather than large. Some few are navigable for short distances for vessels of very light draught. One, the Cauto, draining the triangular valley formed by the Sierra Maestra and the main chain of the island, is navigable for fifty miles to Cauto or El Embarcadero. This is the largest river in the island, but at its mouth is a treacherous bar that was shifted in 1616 by a heavy flood, imprisoning many vessels, including a Spanish man-of-war, all of which had to be abandoned.

Among the other more important rivers may be named the Mantua, Pan de Azúcar Banes, and Marianao, in the province of Pinar del Río; the Chorrera or Almendares (almond groves) is the river which supplies Habana with water, being deflected near the Vento springs by means of an iron aqueduct; the Jatibonico, which empties into the Broa inlet, defines the boundary between the provinces of Matanzas and Santa Clara; the Govea, which empties into the lake of Ariguanabo, and the remarkable Río San Antonio (previously mentioned), which drains the lake and sinks beneath the great Ceiba of San Antonio de los Baños, are in the province of Habana; the Yumurí, the San Juan, and the Canimar, are navigable for short distances and empty into Matanzas Bay; the tortuous Río Palma is navigable for a few miles; the Sagua la Grande, the largest on the north coast, is about 90 miles in length and navigable for 20 miles from its mouth; the Sagua la Chica (little Sagua) rises in the Sierra de Escambray and is navigable for a short distance; the Máximo, emptying into Sabinal Bay, is historically interesting be-

cause it is supposed that at its mouth Columbus disembarked October 27, 1492; the Sara-
maguaca is a copious stream which empties
into the port of Nuevitas. There are also the
Jatibonico del Sur, navigable for 6 or 8 miles;
the Zaza, some 90 miles in length, at whose
mouth is the port of Las Tunas; the Aga-
bama, navigable for a short distance; and the
San Juan, which waters the beautiful plains of
Manicaragua and empties into the bay of
Jagua (Cienfuegos) in the province of Santa
Clara.

In the province of Santiago de Cuba are
the rivers Yarigua, flowing into the port of
Manatí; and many other streams, besides the
Macaguanigua and the Cauto, mentioned
above.

Cuba has few lakes. As a rule these lie
near the coast in close proximity to the
great marshes or everglades. Nevertheless
there are some inclosed among the high
hills of the central chain. Among the latter
none is so remarkable as that of Ariguanabo,
about 20 miles southwest of Habana and near
San Antonio de los Baños. Nestling among
the neighboring ridges, it has a surface of

about six square miles and a depth of thirty feet. It contains fish in large numbers. (See sketch map, p. 19.)

Other lakes there are in the ciénagas of the south coast—torrid quagmires, hidden away from everything except the burning sun, the tropical vegetation, and the loathsome alligators, and known only to the few Cubans who dwell in their vicinity.

THE PLAINS.

The eroded depressions and rolling slopes worn from the mountain chains constitute the main cultivable land of the island and furnish most of the rich, productive soil which, under the stimulus of the southern sun, yields the most plentiful and varied products.

As these low lands compose four-fifths of the area of Cuba (Humboldt), it is readily seen how incalculable must be its wealth. The surface of the interior, gently undulating as in England, rises only from 80 to 100 feet above the level of the ocean. Especially celebrated for their fertility are the districts of Jagua (Cienfuegos), Trinidad, Matanzas, and

Mariel. The valley of Güines owes its celebrity to artificial irrigation (zanjas de riego).

The plains largest in extent are: (1) that occupying the south side of the mountain chain from Pinar del Río to and beyond Güines; (2) that extending from Cárdenas to Holguín; and (3) that of Bayamo (the valley of the Cauto). These are broken, of course, by the groups of mountains and their slopes, but the general elevation is nowhere great, and if a subsidence of a few hundred feet were to take place, everything would disappear beneath the waves of the Atlantic except the mountain groups which have been described as forming the island backbone.

The country may be broadly divided into the region of the plains, the rolling uplands, and the forest lands. The lowlands form a practically continuous belt around the island, and in them are to be found the great sugar plantations. Above these and on the lower slopes are found the grazing and farm lands, upon which, among other things, is raised the famous Habana tobacco. The remainder of the island, especially the eastern portion, is covered with a dense forest growth. — *Scientific American.*

THE COASTS.

The screen of islands, reefs, and banks in front of the Cuban coast covers about

one-half of the perimeter of the island, caus-
ing great inconvenience to navigation, and
making portions of the mainland very difficult of access.   This screen once passed, protection is afforded and navigation made easy.
The reefs are of calcareous origin, and have
been and are still being built by the coral in-
sects, the carcasses of whose ancestors now
form the costal arches of Cuba proper.

Four well-defined locations in front of the
coast are marked by these breakwaters: (1)
From Cape San Antonio to Bahía Honda is
the archipelago of Guaniguanico, which includes the dangerous Bajos de los Colorados, or the Red Banks, the Cayo Inés de
Soto (where fresh water may be obtained),
Cayo Rapado, Santa Isabel, and others; (2)
extending from Cape Hicacos (Cárdenas) to
Nuevitas are the reefs, keys, and banks known
as the Sabana Camaguey, the eastern part
having been called the King's Garden (Jar-
dín del Rey) by Columbus; (3) from Cape
Cruz to Trinidad on the south coast the
shore is fringed and its inclosed waters calmed
by the protection afforded by the archipelago of Los Jardines de la Reina (the queen's
gardens) in which are included the Labe-

rinto de los Doce Leguas (the twelve-league labyrinth), and the Bank of Good Hope (La Buena Esperanza); (4) from Cienfuegos to a point near the western end of the island the south coast is skirted at a considerable distance by the archipelago of the Jardines or Jardinillos (little gardens), including the Isle of Pines. The Jardinillos are the remarkable verdure-clad islets referred to by Réclus as obtaining, through subterranean conduits of rotten (porous) limestone, their fresh water stored many leagues away in the Cuban Highlands.

The portions of the coast sheltered by these archipelagoes are generally marshy, and covered with a thick growth of mangrove and other tropical swamp flora. Frequently they contain, hidden away in their perennial verdure, lakes of fresh, salt, or brackish water. These marshy tracts are known by the general name of Ciénaga (marsh or everglade).

The Ciénaga de Zapata, or shoe-shaped marsh, on the south coast, is one of the largest and most characteristic of these swamps. It has a length of over 60 miles, is perfectly flat, and almost on a level with the sea. The contest between sea and land is here marked, at present, by victories and defeats in about equal proportion; but, in the end, owing to the barrier off this part of the coast, the land must gain by means of its own detritus and with the aid of its tireless coral allies. The stagnant waters of the Ciénaga de Zapata are in places hedged about by sandy breakwaters, and the currentless channels of former rivers are observed here and there among the mangrove thickets, which also are dotted by many lakes, some covered with the leaves of myriad lilies, and others reflecting, as from a mirror, the fiery heat of the southern sun. In some spots the ground is firm enough to support a clump of trees, but most of the surface consists of quagmires or boggy expanses inaccessible to man or beast. The entire coast line from Cienfuegos to Cabo Francés (French cape) is but a continuation of this great swamp.

Where the shore is not hedged about by natural breakwaters (about one-half of the north and one-half of the south coast), the outline presented is high and bold, furnishing many capacious, well-protected harbors with narrow entrances, easy of defense.

Among the fine harbors of the north coast may be mentioned Bahía Honda, Cabañas, Mariel, Habana, Matanzas, Jibara, Nipe, and Baracoa. Those on the south are Guantánamo, Santiago de Cuba, Trinidad, and Cienfuegos.

Some of the keys are inhabited, wherever sufficient fresh water can be obtained upon them, either from the subterranean sources or from the rain water caught in wells or stored in depressions. Many natural salt pans (salinas) are located along their margins, where the salt water is retained in shallow depressions and evaporated by the sun. The salinas along the inlet of Majana, and those of Choco, yield many hundreds of tons of salt annually.

ISLAND OF PINES.

The Island of Pines, named by Columbus " Evangelist Island," belongs to the judicial district of Bejucal. It is about 60 miles from east to west, with a maximum breadth of 55 miles, and an area of about 800 square miles. The population as given by the " Anuario del Comercio " for 1896 is 2000. Communication with the main island is kept up through the port of Batabanó, 60 miles distant.

The principal town is Nueva Gerona,

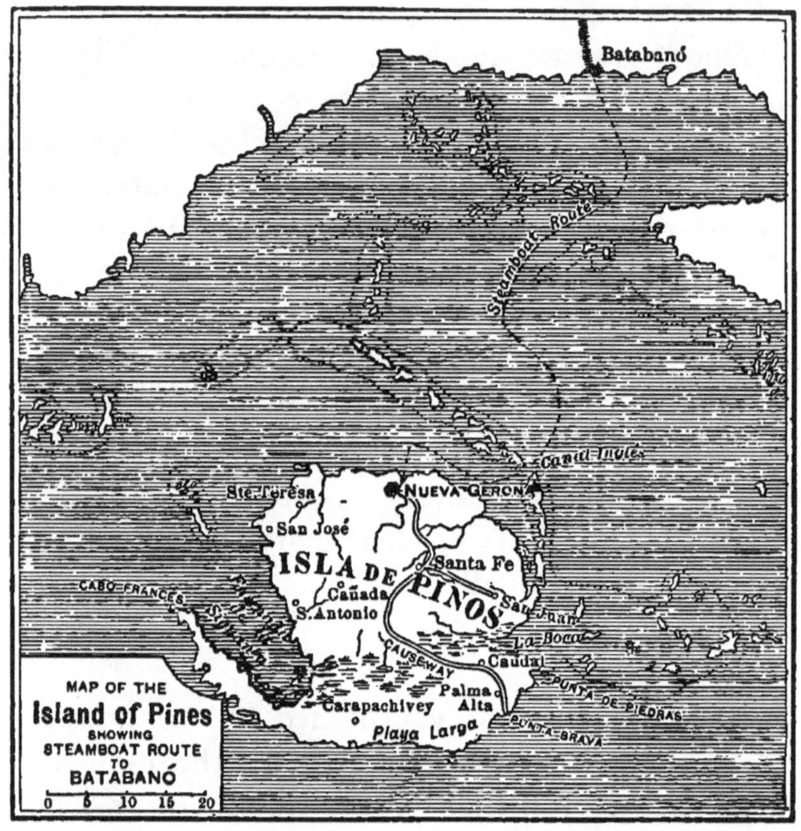

which was founded in 1853, and now has 900 inhabitants. The village of Santa Fe, 14 miles distant, is much frequented on account of its wonderful hot springs.

The Island of Pines consists in reality of two islands separated by a tidal swamp. Toward the eastern end of this swamp a few rocky ledges, flush with the water, have been utilized to construct a stone causeway between the two sections. These present a marked contrast: that on the north is wooded and mountainous, and its soil is extremely fertile; while the southern section is low, rocky, and barren.

The principal products are marble,—many beautiful varieties of which exist in large quantities,—rock crystal, tortoise-shells, pine and turpentine, cedar, mahogany, and other valuable woods. There are also deposits of silver, mercury, and iron.

GEOLOGY.

It is quite well determined in the minds of geologists that Cuba at one time was united to the mainland of the continent, most probably to Florida, during the geological period known as the post-pliocene. Proof of this is to be found in the animal remains,* such as

---

* The fossil animals such as megalonyx, elephants, and hippopotami, found in the miocene rocks of the United States, have also been discovered in the Cuban formations of the same

mastodons and the like, which are found to-day in the Cuban soil where it would not have been possible for them to pass with the present distribution of land and water. An additional proof exists in the similarity and dip of the Cuban rocks and those of the adjacent mainland.*

Fernández de Castro, a noted authority, concludes that in the rocks of the Cuban territory are represented all the great geological divisions. In the western part of the island (Mantua) is a traditional area composed of quartzites and some very dark argillaceous slates, at times carboniferous, containing veins of copper which have been exploited at times. A great part of the central orographical group, where the argillaceous slates and the dark, thin layers alternate with strata of gneiss and talc, appears to belong to the same epoch. Finally, on the north coast, in the Cerro de Dumañuecos, in the vicinity of Manatí, there are great masses

epoch. Hence the inference that at that time the island was connected with the neighboring mainland, and the Gulf Stream must have set in a different direction from its present course.—*Réclus*.

*See note to p. 14.

of quartzite, which should be included in this geological division.

Fernández de Castro is of the opinion that the triassic period is marked by two very extensive layers which, leaving between them a jurassic layer, extend from the southwest of Mantua to the northeast of the San Diego baths. This group is characterized by sandy and variegated loams, full of ferruginous striæ. The jurassic formation is made up of dark-colored limestone and loams, some of which are bituminous. Calcareous spar and black jasper appear at times in the midst of the general mass of the terrain that forms the nucleus of the western orographic zone and extends from the neighborhood of Mantua to Guanajay in a narrow strip some 6 or 7 miles in length. In the Sierra Maestra and in other locations rocks corresponding to this period (jurassic) also appear.

Stratified gray calcareous loams, green clay, greenish limestone, micaceous quartz, and conglomerates are the rocks, which, with marked absence of fossils, characterize the cretaceous deposits of the Island of Cuba.

In the environs of Habana and Guanabacoa, near Vento and Cienfuegos, in a portion of the Sierra Maestra, in the railway cuts from Santiago to Sabanilla and Maroto, in the east of Pinar del Río, in the banks of the Cangre, and at the south of San Diego de los Baños, the cretaceous formation is found. If it appears in other districts it has been but very slightly recognized, if at all, geologically.

With the exception of the above mentioned regions, and of those in which the post-pliocene deposits cover the tertiary strata, these form the larger part of the soil of the island; although perhaps more careful investigations than have thus far been made may force us to include, as belonging to older periods, many zones which are at present assigned to the tertiary.

The three periods, eocene, miocene, and pliocene, appear to be very well marked, as much by their composition as by the abundance of their fossils; for there have been recognized of the latter more than 70 classes and 200 species.

Between Habana and Matanzas are found several banks of argillaceous loams, and some calcareous ones that correspond to the quaternary period, as is testified by their marine fossils, whose species are all living to-day.

The conglomerates of lime, of metamorphic rocks, or of iron, which are so abundant in the island, belong to the same period, as do also the calcareous deposits formed from shell remains, that have accumulated in the neighborhood of Habana, Nuevitas, and Matanzas, and those that are continually formed and appear in the parts of the low coast which the upward movement of the ground is continually exposing.

The vegetable mold, known by the name of Red Earth (tierra colorada), very ferruginous and suitable for the cultivation of coffee and sugar cane, forms the most important of deposits on account of its extent and agricultural value, and is among the most important of the modern period. The ferriferous alluvial masses that are met with between Pinar del Río and Guanajay, between Cárdenas and Sagua la Grande at the south of the Sierra Morena, on the Monte Líbano, and in other places, also belong to the same period. In Pinar del Río, in the cleared tracts of the Vuelta Abajo and in Manicaragua, Trinidad, Mazari, and Yara, important siliceous alluvial deposits exist, which are utilized with remarkable success for the cultivation of tobacco. Of the formations of the present period, the most notable is that of the zoophytic limestone, which is continually transforming the Cuban littoral; increasing it, at times by extending the coast line, and at others by adding to it islets and keys, which in turn are often united to form larger ones, thanks to the constant work of the tireless zoophytes.

Lastly, many other formations might be mentioned, such as the argillaceous alluvia that cover the extensive plains, the deposits of peat, the calcareous tufa, the travertine and the accumulations of detritus from metamorphic rocks; but the great number of these makes it impossible to give a detailed account of them in this brief sketch. The stalactite formations of the celebrated caves of Bellamar in Matanzas and those of Yumurí and Monte Líbano deserve to be mentioned among others.

The hypogenic rocks, granites, syenites, andesites, diorites, euphotites, and serpentines, extraordinarily abundant in the soil of the Island of Cuba, create the belief that the subsoil is made up almost exclusively from them. The serpentine is the most largely exposed, forming a great extent of territory, of a thickness that attains 210 feet in Puerto Príncipe, and 600 in Guanacabuya and Madruga. In it are found rich mines of copper. Native gold abounds in very variable quantities.

CLIMATE.

Considering the tropical position of Cuba, and its slight general elevation, its climate may be regarded as mild.

The seasons are popularly divided into the dry and the wet or rainy, the latter of which extends through the months of May, June, July, August, September, and October. The dampness of the atmosphere averages over 80 per cent. at all seasons, largely due to insular situation.

The temperature in August is from 89° to 91° F.; in December and January, from 70° to 80° F. The mean annual temperature at Habana is 78° F.; for the hottest month, 81° F.; for the coldest, 70° F. (de la Sagra); but refreshing breezes redeem what would otherwise be, during the rainy season, an extremely warm climate, while the dry season may be described as delightful. The prevailing winds are from the north and northwest. The eastern part of the island receives more rain than the western, and the mean annual rainfall is about 40 inches. Hurricanes are frequent and, at long intervals, disastrous, as were those of 1844, 1846, 1865, and 1870. In this respect, however, Cuba is more fortunate than the other Antilles.

METEOROLOGICAL CONDITIONS OF HABANA.

Months.	Temp'ture.	Humidity.	Rainy days.	Rainfall.	Condition of Sky	
					Cloudy Days.	Clear Days.
January......	71° F.	82. %	8	2.5 in.	5	26
February....	74° "	84. %	7	2.1 "	8	20
March	74° "	82.8 %	6	2.4 "	7	24
April........	76° "	82.4 %	4	1.2 "	5	25
May.........	78° "	85.4 %	8	3.6 "	8	23
June........	81° "	85. %	10	5.1 "	6	24
July........	82° "	87.6 %	12	5.6 "	6	25
August......	82° "	88.2 %	12	4.8 "	6	25
September...	80° "	88.2 %	14	6. "	7	23
October.....	79° "	85.2 %	9	3.2 "	7	24
November...	75° "	86.2 %	8	3.3 "	8	22
December...	73° "	84.8 %	6	1.2 "	7	24
Means or Totals.	77° F.	85.15 %	104	41.0 in.	80	285

It is necessary to say, in this connection, that the incomplete data and observations made upon Cuban territory render it impossible to give much detailed or even very exact information concerning the climate. It is thought, however, that the preceding table from the " Historia física, política y natural de la Isla de Cuba," by de la Sagra, will be found useful.

According to the same authority the highest temperature observed at Habana during a long period was 32° C. (90° F.), and the minimum 10° C. (50° F.)

The coldest month is January and the warmest, August, with only a difference of 6° C. (23° F.). In the interior of the island local causes, such as the proximity of forests or mountains, or the greater or less barrenness of the terrain, influence the temperature, giving results different from those experienced at Habana.

Rarely are there more than 20 rainy days in any one month, and the average is from 8 to 10. The rainfall is generally in the afternoon, and on an average there are only 17 days in the year in which it rains in both forenoon and afternoon.

Such effects with the splendid sun, the few completely cloudy days, copious rains in the warmest season and abundant breezes when the rains fail, make Cuba for vegetation a terrestrial paradise, and for climate, one of the best, if not the very best, of intertropical regions.

The visitor from the far north is at once impressed with the distinctness of distant objects—due to the great transparency of the atmosphere. At night, too, the appearance of the sky is far more beautiful than in northern countries, and the air does not seem to lose its transparency with the departure of day. On the open plains the light of the stars alone is usually sufficient for the traveler. The sunsets are remarkable for their soft, mellow glow, all too brief for the eye accustomed to the lingering twilight of northern climes. The sea is incomparably beautiful—deep green with shifting coppery lights, like liquid opal. Northern skies are never reflected in waters of such fanciful hues, and were an artist to depict them truthfully he would be declared color-mad.

PRODUCTS.

The Cuban soil possesses all the strength and characteristics due to its position in the torrid zone, and is so fertile that two crops of some cereals are frequently obtained in the same year. The foliage is green at all seasons, but, notwithstanding the exuberance of the tropical vegetation, the landscapes often present an arid appearance owing to the almost total absence of grass-covered fields and hillsides.

The mineral products of Cuba have not attracted much attention, although rich ore deposits exist in many parts of the island.

Copper occurs in the extreme eastern and western departments, Santiago de Cuba and Pinar del Río. The mines at present in operation are in the former province, 12 miles out of Santiago de Cuba, and support a mining population of over 2000. The daily yield is several tons, the larger and more valuable pieces of the ore being shipped direct to Europe, while the smaller and poorer are smelted at the mines.

Bituminous coal of fine quality, yielding little ash, is found in large quantities in many parts of the island, from the coast to the mountains. That found near the coast is often in a viscous state.

Marble of many varieties and of fine quality is abundant, and is distributed through most of the provinces, the Island of Pines being especially favored.

Gold is found in the central provinces, at Sagua la Grande, in the banks of the Holguín, and other rivers. But at this date there is no reason to suppose that Cuba will ever assume importance as a gold producer.

Iron ore, yielding a metal that makes a superb quality of steel, is mined in the province of Santiago de Cuba, especially in the immediate vicinity of its capital. At Alto Songo, 19 miles from Santiago de Cuba, manganese is exploited. At Juragua, Caney, and Cobre (12 miles from Santiago de Cuba) several different classes of ores are found.

The mines reported in Cuba (1891-92) were as follows:

Of iron, ...	138
" manganese, ...	88
" copper, ...	53

The chief wealth of the island is, however, in its agricultural products, the principal of which are sugar, tobacco, and coffee.

The first sugar plantation was established in 1595; but the industry did not assume prime importance until the present century.

In addition to the burden of heavy taxation, the trade has of late years suffered severely from competition with beet sugar. The yield in 1894--95 was 1,040,000 tons, with an estimated addition of 400,000 tons of molasses and an unknown quantity of rum. The falling off in the quantity sent to Great Britain is remarkable, being from Cuba and Puerto Rico:

In	1879 of the value of .		.	.	$6,290,856
"	1880 " " " "	.	.	.	3,730,058
"	1888 " " " "	.	.	.	1,079,049
"	1890 " " " "	.	.	.	75,983
"	1892 " " " "	.	.	.	46,706

Tobacco is indigenous in Cuba, and its quality is so universally known that it need not be spoken of at length here. The export for 1892 was 240,000 bales and 166,712,000 cigars.

Coffee was introduced by the French into Martinique in 1727, but did not make its appearance in Cuba until 1769, 42 years later. It was the revolution in Santo Domingo that gave the first great stimulus to coffee-raising in Cuba. The refugees from Santo Domingo sought shelter wherever they could among the nearest islands, and large numbers settled in the eastern end of Cuba. Here they turned into smiling gardens lands that had been idle for centuries, and the production of the favorite berry became very profitable for a number of years, many cargoes being shipped annually to the United States from the ports of Trinidad and Santiago. Coffee no longer figures to any extent in the statistics of exports. Exorbitant taxation and the ravages of civil war, in the coffee districts especially, are largely the cause of the loss of an important and profitable industry.

According to statistics furnished by the New York Chamber of Commerce, the amount of coffee produced in Cuba during the ten years prior to 1885 was 24,000 cwt., as compared with 192,500 cwt. in Puerto Rico, 1,400,000 cwt. in Java and Sumatra, and 4,250,000 cwt. in Brazil.

The low lands on the coast are admirably adapted to the growth of the fine sea-island cotton. Maize, or Indian corn, peppers, yams, and sweet potatoes are raised for home use. Almost all the fruits of the tropics and subtropics grow freely, as the pineapple, the orange, the plantain, the banana, the fig, and the pomegranate. Cocoa, cassava, honey, and wax are produced both for home consumption and for export.

The dense, uncleared forests of Cuba are estimated at 13,000,000 acres, abounding in tropical and other valuable woods, including mahogany, ebony, cedar, sabicú, and granadillo.

All of the large trees of the Mexican coast, so remarkable for their majestic growth, for the beauty of their foliage, the splendor and fragrance of their flowers, reappear on the Cuban seaboard. Over thirty species of palms are here met with in association with trees such as the pine, which seems so characteristic of the temperate zone and which gives its name to the Isla de Pinos, where it is found intermingled with palms and mahogany. The botanical catalogue of 1876 enumerates altogether 3350 indigenous flowering plants, besides those introduced by Europeans.

COMMUNICATIONS.

The communications (by road, railway, and boat) have never been good or sufficient. The roads themselves, as a rule, are mere trails, and in the wet season are in a deplorable condition.

Wagon Roads.—The most famous is called the Camino Central (or the Central road), and runs from Habana to Santiago de Cuba, passing through Luyanó, San Miguel del Padrón, Santa María del Rosario, Jaruco, Limonar, Guamutas, Ceja de Pablo, Alvarez, Esperanza, Santa Clara, Santo Espíritu, Ciego de Avila, Puerto Príncipe, Tunas, Bayamo, Jiguaní, and Palma Soriano.

A calzada is a paved highway, or turnpike; and of these there are the following, all of which have been constructed at the expense of the Government (*i. e.*, have been paid for from the Cuban budget):

Coloma to Pinar del Río, ...	15 miles
Habana to San Cristóbal, and thence to Pinar del Río, ...	60 "
(N. B.—From Habana to Guanajay this road is called the Western Calzada; and from the latter point to its terminus it is known as the Southwestern Calzada.)	
Habana to Bejucal, called the Southern Calzada, ...	15 "
Batabanó to the beach, ...	$2\frac{1}{8}$ "
Habana to Güines, known as the Southeastern Calzada, ...	30 "

Habana to Santa María del Rosario, . . 15 miles
Luyanó to the eastern outskirts of Guana-
    bacoa, called the Eastern Calzada, . 12 "
      (N. B.—It is proposed to extend this
   road to Matanzas.)
Núñez to La Canoa, ... 26 "

In addition there are numerous short calzadas built by the municipalities of the towns which they benefit.

Outside the cities the universal passenger vehicle is the *volante* (" flyer "), which consists of a two-seated carriage slung rather low down, by leather straps, from the axle of two very large wheels, and having shafts 15 feet long. The horse in the shafts is led by a postilion, whose horse is also harnessed to the carriage with traces. In the case of a long and rough journey, a third horse is harnessed on the other side of the shafts in the same manner. This carriage is extremely comfortable to travel in, and the great height of the wheels and their distance apart prevent all danger of turning over—a very desirable attribute in view of the condition of most of the roads in the interior.

Merchandise, when not sent by rail, is usually transported by heavy carts drawn by oxen or mules. Pack mules are employed where the roads cannot be used by the carts.

Railroads.—The railway lines of Cuba, comprising upward of 1000 miles of track, are controlled by the 10 companies enumerated below. In addition there are numerous private roads (mostly narrow-gauge), which have been built by the sugar planters to connect their estates with the main lines. The public railroads now in operation are as follows:

(1) The United Railways Co. (Ferrocarriles Unidos), with four lines: (*a*) Habana to Matanzas, (*b*) Habana to Batabanó, (*c*) Habana to La Unión, (*d*) Habana to Guanajay. The lines of this company traverse the most populous districts of the island, and by their junction with other lines most of the remaining railway points in Cuba can be reached.

(2) The Western Railway (Ferrocarril Occidente) traverses the Vuelta Abajo tobacco district, reaching the city of Pinar del Río, 106 miles southwest from Habana.

(3) The Cárdenas and Júcaro Railway (Ferrocarril Cárdenas-Júcaro), with main line from Cárdenas to Santa Clara.

(4) The Matanzas Railway (Ferrocarril de Matanzas) with (*a*) line from Matanzas to Murga, (*b*) line from Matanzas to Guaveiras.

(5) The Sagua la Grande Railway (Ferrocarril Sagua la Grande), line from Concha to Cruces.

(6) The Cienfuegos and Santa Clara Railway (Ferrocarril Cienfuegos-Santa Clara).

(7) The Caibarién United Railways (Ferrocarriles Unidos de Caibarién), with line from Caibarién to Placetas.

(8) The Puerto Príncipe and Nuevitas Railway (Ferrocarril de Puerto Príncipe-Nuevitas) connecting the capital of the province with its port.

(9) The Guantánamo Railway (Ferrocarril de Guantánamo).

(10) The Marianao Railway (Ferrocarril de Marianao), a short suburban line of $8\frac{1}{2}$ miles, connecting Habana with Marianao and La Playa, used chiefly for passenger traffic.

Eventually, doubtless, there will be continuous railway communication from Pinar del Río to Santiago de Cuba, approximately following the axis of the island, touching at Habana, Santa Clara, Santo Espíritu,

Puerto Príncipe, Las Tunas, and Holguín, and throwing off branches to all important harbors, ports, and towns not touched by the main line.

Steamers.—There are frequent coastwise and foreign steamers connecting Cuban coast towns with each other and with the outer world. The steamers of the Línea Transatlántica ply between Habana and Cadiz, Santander, and Coruña, at intervals of 10 days. There is a monthly steamer between Vera Cruz and Southampton, stopping at St. Thomas and at Habana. A French line runs from Saint Nazaire to Habana, stopping at Santander. There are regular lines from Habana to Sisal and Vera Cruz; from Habana to Colón, stopping at Nuevitas and Jibara; from Habana to Puerto Rico, stopping at all the principal Cuban ports of the north coast; a French line from Habana to Vera Cruz and New Orleans; a German line from Habana to Hamburg; and a steamer running twice a week between Habana and Key West.

The following are the steamship lines from New York to Habana:

New York and Cuba Mail Steamship Co.,

for Habana every Wednesday and Saturday. Steamers *Segurança*, Habana and Mexican ports; *Saratoga*, Habana and Tampico; *Seneca*, Habana and Mexican ports. For Nassau, Santiago, and Cienfuegos, via Guantánamo, every alternate Thursday, Steamer *Santiago*. Jas. E. Ward & Co., agents, 113 Wall Street, New York.

Munson Steamship Line from New York for Matanzas, Cárdenas, and Sagua, Steamers *Ardanmohr*, *Ardanrose*, and *Ardandhu*. Also from Philadelphia for Habana, Tampico, and Vera Cruz, Steamer *Vittoria*. W. D. Munson, 80 Wall Street, New York.

Compañía Transatlántica Española (formerly A. López & Co., North American Branch, under contract with the Spanish Government). Steamers leave New York for Habana direct on the 10th, 20th, and 30th of every month. J. M. Ceballos & Co., agents, pier 10, East River.

Bea Bellido & Co. line of steamers for Matanzas, Cárdenas, Sagua, and Caibarién. Waydell & Co., 21 Old Slip.

Regular line for Guantánamo, Santiago, and Cienfuegos. Steamer *Ardangorm* Waydell & Co., 21 Old Slip.

Coastwise steamers ply, with more or less regularity, between Habana and Cárdenas; Habana, Sagua, and Caibarién; Habana and Santiago de Cuba, calling at Nuevitas, Jibara, Baracoa, and Guantánamo; Batabanó and Santiago, landing at Cienfuegos, Trinidad, Las Tunas, Santa Cruz, and Manzanillo; Batabanó and the Isle of Pines; Batabanó and Bailén, calling at Dayaniguas, Coloma, Colón, Punta de Cartas, and Laguna de Cortés; Habana and San Cayetano, landing at Bahía Honda.

Cable and Telegraph.—The only towns in Cuba having cable connections are Habana, Cienfuegos, and Santiago de Cuba.

The International Ocean Telegraph Co. has a cable from Habana to Florida in connection with the Western Union Telegraph Co. of the United States.

The Cuba Submarine Telegraph Co. (Limited) has a cable connecting Habana with Santiago de Cuba and Cienfuegos.

The West India and Panama Telegraph Co. has a cable connecting Habana with Santiago de Cuba, Jamaica, Puerto Rico, the Lesser Antilles, and the Isthmus of Panama.

The Compagnie Française de Câbles Sous-Marins has a cable connecting Habana with Santiago de Cuba, Haití, Santo Domingo, Venezuela, and Brazil.

The telegraph system in Cuba is in the hands of the Government. There are wires connecting all the principal towns and villages in the island.

Telephones.—The telephone system in Habana also belongs to the Government, but is farmed out for a limited number of years to a company called the *Red Telefónica de la Habana.* Nearly all the public and private buildings in the city and suburbs are connected by telephone.

GAZETTEER OF THE ISLAND OF CUBA.

PROVINCES.

Cuba is politically divided into six provinces. The name of the province and of its chief city is in each instance the same. Each province is divided into several judicial districts, whose names are important to the reader because events are often said to take place in a certain district, while the province is not named. The tract of country surrounding, and pertaining to, each town, will be called a township. The provinces, taken in order from west to east, are: Pinar del Río, Habana, Matanzas, Santa Clara, Puerto Príncipe, and Santiago de Cuba.

Pinar del Río is the famous tobacco region whose choice products are usually bought up in advance by speculators and retailed at exorbitant prices to European potentates and other wealthy customers. The less important agricultural products are sugar, coffee, rice, corn, cotton, and fruits. Communications with Habana and throughout the province are abundant and good.

Habana.—This important province yields all the various agricultural products of the island, and is the principal manufacturing center. Coal is exploited to a small extent.

Matanzas, a center of sugar production, is one of the richest and most developed portions of the island. It produces also corn, rice, fruits, honey, and wax. Peat is found, and mines of copper have been worked.

Santa Clara, formerly called Las Cinco Villas (the five towns) on account of the five towns founded within its limits by Diego Velázquez, is one of the richest, as it was one of the first settled, parts of the island. It contains some of the largest sugar plantations and factories. Its rich soil yields in abundance all the special products of the Antilles; and the fruits of the temperate zone thrive on the elevated slopes of its mountain ranges. It is rich too in minerals, furnishing silver, copper, and asphalt; and gold has been found in the sands of the Arimo river.

Puerto Príncipe includes the part of the island often referred to as Camagüey, which was formerly the central department. It is a mountainous region, and contains immense forests, still in a state of nature. Here too are the largest caves in Cuba; and in the inaccessible heights of this province the present insurgents have fixed their temporary capital. The principal industries are the cutting of building and cabinet woods and the preparation of preserves of guava. The province has suffered from being repeatedly the seat of insurrection.

Santiago de Cuba.—This large and wealthy province abounds in all that distinguishes the others, and in mineral riches surpasses them all. Its mountains contain gold, copper, iron, manganese, mercury, zinc, asphalt, marble, alabaster, rock crystal, and gems. Its commerce enlivens the ports of Mayari, Gibara, Baracoa, Cuba (Santiago de Cuba) Guantánamo, and Manzanillo.

DISTRICTS INTO WHICH THE SIX PROVINCES ARE DIVIDED.

Name.	Population.	Province in which situated.
Alfonso XII.,	33,887	Matanzas.
Baracoa,	18,057	Santiago de Cuba.
Bejucal,	43,709	Habana.
Cárdenas,	53,882	Matanzas.
Cienfuegos,	72,187	Santa Clara.
Colón,	79,390	Matanzas.
Guanabacoa,	32,344	Habana.
Guanajay,	59,348	Pinar del Río.
Guane,	56,393	Pinar del Río.
Guantánamo,	30,044	Santiago de Cuba.
Güines,	45,577	Habana.
Habana,	213,500	Habana.
Holguín,	58,900	Santiago de Cuba.
Jaruco,	38,403	Habana.
Juan de los Remedios,	15,358	Santa Clara.
Manzanillo,	25,735	Santiago de Cuba.
Marianao,	7,352	Habana.
Matanzas,	86,249	Matanzas.
Morón,	57,620	Puerto Príncipe.
Pinar del Río,	70,565	Pinar del Río.
Puerto Príncipe,	66,457	Puerto Príncipe.
Sagua la Grande,	79,126	Santa Clara.
San Antonio de los Baños,	32,961	Habana.
San Cristóbal,	44,700	Pinar del Río.
Santiago de Cuba,	62,600	Santiago de Cuba.

Aguacate, province of Habana, 13 miles from Jaruco, population, 1427; of township, 4028.

Alfonso XII., province of Matanzas, 13 miles from Matanzas, population, 3000.

Alonso Rojas, province of Pinar del Río, 28 miles from Pinar del Río, population, 200; of township, 4156.

Alquizar, province of Habana, population, 2700; of township, 8700.

Alto Songo, province of Santiago de Cuba, 19 miles from that city, population, 400; of township, 12,000.

Amaro, province of Santa Clara, population, 320; of township, 7251.

Artemisa, province of Pinar del Río, 10 miles from Guanajay, population, 4587; of township, 9286.

Bahía Honda, province of Pinar del Río, population, 1889; of township, 8534. Has one of the finest harbors in Cuba.

Bainoa, province of Habana, 8 miles from Jaruco, population, 1000; of township, 3500.

Bajo, province of Pinar del Río, population, 164; of township, 4393.

Baracoa, province of Santiago de Cuba,

the first city laid out in Cuba (1512); population, 5213; of township, 18,092. The principal products are bananas and cocoa, and the oil of the latter. The caves in the vicinity are remarkable for their stalactites and fossil human remains.

Batabanó, province of Habana, 45 miles from the capital, population, 1864; of township, 8518.

Bayamo, province of Santiago de Cuba, 94 miles from that city, population, 3634; of township, 17,719.

Bejucal, province of Habana, 21 miles from the capital, population, 6239; of township, 8972.

Bemba (see Jovellanos).

Bolondrón, province of Matanzas, 29 miles from Habana, population, 1758; of township, 11,816.

Cabañas, province of Pinar del Río, population, 1509; of township, 8650. It is situated near a fine bay, whose narrow entrance is guarded by Fort Reina Amalia.

Caibarién, province of Santa Clara, population, 5300; of township, 8128—has a good harbor.

Calabazar, province of Santa Clara, population, 1481; of township, 8898.

Camerones, province of Santa Clara, 16 miles from Cienfuegos, population, 546; of township, 8600.

Canasí, province of Matanzas, 17 miles from that city, population, 700; of township, 8600.

Candelaria, province of Pinar del Río, 6 miles from San Cristóbal, population, 1200; of township, 6300. Noted for its mineral springs and the excellence of its coffee.

Caney, province of Santiago de Cuba, population, 700; of township, 8600.

Cárdenas, province of Matanzas, 30 miles from that city, population, 20,505; of township, 33,882. It is a rich and handsome city with flourishing trade and manufactures of liquors, soaps, cigars, etc.

Cartagena, province of Santa Clara, 24 miles from Cienfuegos, population, 1497; of township, 8915.

Catalina, province of Habana, 45 miles from the capital, population, 1165; of township, 7000.

Cayajalos, province of Pinar del Río, 12

miles from Guanajay, population, 1352; of township, 8129.

Ceiba del Agua, province of Habana, 3 miles from San Antonio de los Baños, population, 892; of township, 3252.

Cervantes, province of Matanzas, 12 miles from Colón, population, 1560; of township, 4000.

Cidra, province of Matanzas, 3 miles from Santa Ana, population, 695; of township, 4170.

Ciego de Avila, province of Puerto Príncipe, population, 1167; of township, 7000. It occupies the central position on the old Trocha, or military line of defense.

Cienfuegos, province of Santa Clara, population, 26,790; of township, 41,000. This is a modern city, built on the fine harbor of Jagua, and is one of the richest and most beautiful in the island.

Cimarrones, province of Matanzas, 13 miles from Cárdenas, population, 300; of township, 8746.

Colón, province of Matanzas, 84 miles from that city, population 6525; of township, 16,679—the heart of the sugar-producing region.

Consolación del Sur, province of Pinar del Río, 4 miles from the city of that name, population, 2000; of township, 16,057. It is the second city of the province in importance. Has over 800 plantations of the finest tobacco.

Corral Nuevo, province of Matanzas, population, 2092; of township, 12,575.

Cuevitas, province of Matanzas, 20 miles from Colón, population, 1629; of township, 6551.

Gibara, province of Santiago de Cuba, population, 4608; of township, 26,844. The town has a magnificent harbor on the north coast, admitting vessels of 16 feet draft. Its trade is in sugar, coffee, tobacco, fruits, and native woods.

Guana, province of Habana, 8 miles from Güines, population, 4650; of township, 13,950.

Guanabacoa, suburb of Habana, population, 11,144.

Guanajay, province of Pinar del Río, 26 miles from Habana, population, 5792; of township, 9491.

Guanajayabo, province of Matanzas, population, 2879; of township, 8132.

Guane, province of Pinar del Río, 28 miles from the town of that name, population, 510; of township, 5000.

Guantánamo, province of Santiago de Cuba, population, 9000; of township, 24,000. The bay is one of the finest on the coast.

Guira de Melena, province of Habana, population, 3500; of township, 9500.

Habana is the chief city of the province of that name and the capital of the whole island. It has a population of 200,000, which, however, is subject to fluctuations. It contains many fine buildings, of which the most conspicuous is the cathedral, where repose the mortal remains of Columbus and of his son Diego. There are also the university of Habana, the residences of the Governor General and the bishop, three theaters and a number of educational and eleemosynary institutions. The opera house is one of the most magnificent in the world, and, with the great number of private carriages, indicates the wealth and luxurious tastes of the inhabitants. There is a botanical garden, and of the two public squares one is widely celebrated for its size and beauty. The streets are generally narrow, but the

promenade of Isabel Segunda, which traverses the center of the city, is very fine, having
a broad carriage-way in the center and
shaded walks on either side. It is also en-
livened by fountains, of which there are 50
in the city.

For a long time the houses were kept low
through fear of earthquakes; but now the
greater number are of two stories, while
some are much higher. The city is accom-
modated by two separate systems of street
railways.

In peaceful and prosperous times the
amount of business handled, both in trade
and manufactures, is very great. Nearly all
commercial nations have representative
houses here; and the powers of the Governor
General are so nearly regal that foreign
consuls have to exercise diplomatic functions.
As many as 3000 vessels enter and clear in a
year. The spacious harbor, if dredged in the
parts that are slowly filling up, would
shelter the navies of the world. It is provided with a floating dock, and is fringed
with warehouses, wharves, and gaudy bathing houses.

The principal defenses of Habana are the

Castillo de la Punta to the west of the harbor entrance, the Castillo del Morro and San Carlos de la Cabaña to the east, the Santo Domingo de Atarés, which lies at the head of the western arm of the bay and commands

CASTILLO DEL MORRO, AS SEEN FROM LA PUNTA.

both the city and the neighborhood, and the Castillo del Príncipe, situated on an eminence to the west, and forming the terminus of the great Paseo Militar. El Morro, as it is popularly called, was first erected in 1589, but additions have been frequently made. La Punta, a much smaller fort, is of the same period. The castle of Atarés dates from about 1763, when the Conde de Ricla was Governor of the island. Cabaña, which alone has accommodation for 4000 men, fronts the bay for a distance of 800 yards, and is defended on the land side by three bastions. To the east there lies a smaller fort, No. 4, or San Diego, on a hill about 100 feet high.

The relative importance of these fortifications is apparent from the rank of the commanding officer of each, as given in the Spanish Army List for 1895:

Castillo del Príncipe, commanded by a Brigadier General.

Castillo de la Cabaña, commanded by a Brigadier General.

Fuerte de San Diego, commanded by a First Lieutenant of Infantry.

Castillo del Morro, commanded by a Major of Infantry.

Castillo de la Punta, commanded by a Captain of Infantry.

Castillo de Atarés, commanded by a First Lieutenant of Infantry.

Batería de la Reina, commanded by a Captain of Artillery.

Batería de Santa Clara, commanded by a Captain of Artillery.

Holguín, province of Santiago de Cuba, 175 miles from the city of that name, population, 5418; of township, 32,056.

Jaruco, province of Habana, 34 miles from the capital, population, 2145; of township, 12,584.

Jibacoa, province of Habana, 12 miles from Jaruco, population, 696; of township, 3966.

Jiguane, province of Santiago de Cuba, 18 miles from Bayamo, population, 1393; of township, 8033.

Jovellanos (popularly known as Bemba), province of Matanzas, 20 miles from Colón, population, 6000; of township, 9000.

La Esperanza, province of Santa Clara, population, 2147; of township, 10,733. The township comprises 15 settlements, 92 grazing farms, and 647 under cultivation.

Lagunillas, province of Matanzas, 7 miles from Cárdenas, population, 520; of township, 7030.

Limonar, province of Matanzas, population, 330; of township, 2000.

Macagua, province of Matanzas, population, 4100; of township, 13,410. This township is distinguished for its great sugar estates.

Macuriges, province of Matanzas, population, 3650; of township, 13,500.

Madruga, province of Habana; a bathing

resort (warm springs), 52 miles from the capital.

Managua, province of Habana, 16 miles from Guanabacoa, population, 896; of township, 5860.

Mangas, province of Pinar del Río, population, 209; of township, 3576.

Mantua, province of Pinar del Río, population, 1380; of township, 8000.

Manzanillo, province of Santiago de Cuba, 160 miles from that city, population, 9036; of township, 25,735. The town is situated on a fine bay; the township produces annually more than 30,000 tons of sugar, besides the products of the forests.

Marianao, 6 miles from Habana, population, 1225; of township, 7352.

Mariel, province of Pinar del Río, 8 miles from Guanajay, population, 1637; of township, 9207. The town has a fine harbor.

Matanzas, capital of the rich province of the same name, and the second commercial city of the island. It is distant from Habana 74 miles by rail, or 54 by wagon road. Population 50,000. Matanzas is situated on a magnificent bay, where the rivers San Juan and Yumurí enter, dividing it into three parts. The part between the rivers is the oldest; the northern section is called Versalles, and the southern Pueblo Nuevo (new town). The buildings that chiefly attract attention are the Estabán theater—one of the finest in America—the Casino and the Lyceum. Among the principal resorts are La Plaza de Armas, Eremita de Monserrat, the boulevard de Santa Cristina, and the beautiful park in the valley of the Yumurí. That tropical valley is one of surpassing natural beauty.

Three and a half miles out of the city are the beautiful caves of Bellamar, opening upon the bay. This is a great resort for sea bathing, and the beaches are inclosed by iron gratings to exclude the sharks that infest Cuban waters. The natural beauty of the crystallizations in these caves has been greatly impaired by guides carrying smoky torches. The fine hotel at the entrance has recently been burned by the insurrectionists.

Melena del Sur, province of Habana, distant 8 miles from Güines, population, 1082; of township, 5275.

Morón, province of Puerto Príncipe, 85

miles from the city of that name, population, 3017; of the township, 7870. Its exports are tobacco, sugar, cedar, mahogany, and ebony.

Nueva Paz, province of Habana, population, 2737; of township, 9571.

Palmillas, province of Matanzas, population, 1471; of twnship, 8818.

Palmira, province of Santa Clara, 9 miles from Cienfuegos, population, 2987; of township, 4995.

Pinar del Río, capital of the province of that name, 155 miles southwest from Habana. It is the center of the famous tobacco district, is connected by a turnpike with its seaport, Coloma, and has a population of 5500.

Puerto Príncipe, capital of the province of that name, near the center of which it is located. Its seaport is Nuevitas, which was called Puerto Príncipe by Columbus. Its present site was selected in 1516, where the Indian village of Camagüey then was. The usual communication with Habana is by railway to Nuevitas, and thence by steamer. Population, 40,679; of township, 55,459.

Quemados de Güines, province of Santa Clara, 12 miles from Sagua la Grande, population, 2000; of township, 14,000.

Quivicán, province of Habana, center of a cattle district, close to Bejucal, population, of town, 1950; of township, 5600.

Rancho Veloz, province of Santa Clara 25 miles from Sagua la Grande, population, 656; of township, 8237.

Ranchuela, province of Santa Clara, 28 miles from Cienfuegos, population, 1533; of township, 10,733.

Regla, a suburb of Habana, reached by ferry; population, 10,486. It has a famous bull-ring.

Roque, province of Matanzas, population, 800; of township, 6750. Produces sugar, coffee, and bananas.

Sabanilla del Encomendador, province of Matanzas, population, 2991; of township, 8871.

Sagua la Grande, province of Santa Clara, 260 miles from Habana, population, 14,000; of township, 23,740. It is one of the most important cities on the island, and is connected by railway with Habana, Santa Clara, and Cienfuegos.

Sagua de Tánamo, province of Santiago de Cuba, 125 miles from that city, population, 981; of township, 6044.

Salud, province of Habana, 5 miles from Bejucal, population, 800; of township, 4970.

San Antonio de Cabezas, province of Matanzas, population, 1500; of township, 10,200.

San Antonio de las Vegas, province of Habana, 13 miles from Bejucal, population, 1136; of township, 4600.

San Antonio de los Baños, province of Habana, 21 miles from the capital, population, 7500; of township, 11,730. The city takes its name from the mineral springs that empty into the river that drains the wonderful lake Ariguanabo, already mentioned under the head of " Water Courses."

San Antonio de Río Blanco del Norte, province of Habana, population, 1200; of township, 5800.

San Cristóbal, province of Pinar del Río, 70 miles from Habana, population, 3522; of township, 17,610.

San Diego del Valle, province of Santa Clara, population, 1403; of township, 9820.

San Felipe, province of Habana, population, 2311; of township, 9244.

San Fernando de Nuevitas, province of Puerto Príncipe, is the port for the capital of that province; population, 6,991.

San José de las Lajas, province of Habana, 18 miles from the capital, population 2170; of township, 7000.

San José de los Ramos, province of Matanzas, 12 miles from Colón, population, 570; of township, 9500.

San Juan de los Remedios, province of Santa Clara, 4 miles from Caibarién and 295 from Habana, population, 7230; of township, 15,550. The town was founded in 1545, on an islet or " key," and afterward removed. Its port is Caibarién.

San Juan de las Yevas, province of, and 14 miles from, Santa Clara; population, 2267; of township, 7808.

San Juan y Martínez, province of Pinar del Río, population, 2100; of township, 19,000.

San Julián de los Güines (or, simply, Güines), province of Habana; distant from the capital 30 miles by wagon road and 45 by rail. This city is the center of a rich sugar district; population, 6828; of township, 12,401. The

Catalina river traverses the town and is crossed by ten bridges.

San Luis, province of Pinar del Río, distant from that city 10 miles; population, 3556; of township, 9125.

San Matías de Río Blanco, a village of 400 inhabitants, near San Antonio de Río Blanco del Norte; its port is frequented by coasting vessels.

San Miguel, a bathing village 11 miles from Limonar in the province of Matanzas.

San Nicolás, province of Habana, 9 miles from Güines, population, 1100; of township, 6680.

Santa Ana, province of Matanzas, 7 miles from that city, population, 601; of township, 8239.

Santa Clara, capital of the province of that name. Its popular designation is Villa Clara. It is 248 miles from Habana, and has a population of 34,635. The city has a fine theater. There is considerable mineral wealth in its vicinity. Gold, plumbago, and copper have been found; there is a gasoline mine a mile and a quarter from the city, and as much as 10,000 tons of superior asphaltum has been shipped in a single year.

Santa Cruz del Sur, province of Puerto Príncipe, population, 1000; of township, 4016. The chief products are cedar, mahogany, honey, wax, cattle, and turtles' eggs.

Santa Isabel de las Lajas, province of Santa Clara, 31 miles from Cienfuegos, population, 4924; of township, 9104. It has a large and increasing commerce, in which the leading articles are sugar and cattle.

Santa María del Rosario, province of Habana, $3\frac{1}{2}$ miles from the capital, population, 660; of township, 4854. Noted for its mineral springs.

Santiago de Cuba (often called merely Cuba), capital of the province of the same name, founded in 1514 by Diego Velásquez, on the southeast coast, and was for a long time the capital of the island. It is situated on a fine harbor, whose narrow entrance is defended by two forts. It has some notable buildings; especially the cathedral, built in 1522. Owing to its inclosed situation, the atmosphere is close and stifling, and the place is not healthy. It is the second commercial port in the island; its principal exports are liquors, hides, cocoa, coffee, tobacco, guavas, and pineapples.

Santiago de las Vegas, 11 miles from Habana, population 6000; of township, 11,000.

Santo Domingo, province of Santa Clara, population, 1750; of township, 17,000; the principal business is farming and grazing.

Santo Espíritu (also known as Sancti Spíritus), province of Santa Clara, distant 55 miles from the city of that name; population, 17,540; of township, 500.

Tapaste, province of Habana, situated on the great central wagon-road of the island, and the center of considerable trade; population, 1130; of the township, 6125.

Vereda Nueva, province of Santa Clara, population, 672; of township, 4000.

Viñales, province of Pinar del Río, from that city distant 16 miles, population, 925; of township, 11,727. Near the town are the celebrated San Vicente mineral springs.

PART II

HISTORICAL.

By M. M. RAMSEY, A. M.

CHAPTER I.

IN tracing the course of maritime enterprise, the discoveries of the Phœnicians and the Northmen may be passed over, as premature and productive of no valuable results. In that development of exploration which has continued to the present time, the Portuguese were the pioneers.

The chief object from the days of Hiram and Solomon to the sixteenth century was always a route to India and the fabulous wealth of the East. In the thirteenth century the Polos penetrated eastward far beyond the turning points of all previous explorers, remained many years at the court of the great Kublai Khan, reached Peking, and heard of an empire, Zipangri—now recognized as Japan—still farther east. Upon their return, and the publication of Marco Polo's narrative, the thinking part of Europe was roused and given a new subject of thought to take the place of the seven lost crusades. About the same time the compass began to be known and used by Europeans, and made mariners less dependent on the shore and the stars. Another impulse was given by the fact that about 1334 a French ship, driven from her course, accidentally discovered the Canary Islands, which had been heard of but not seen by the Romans.

It was the fortune of Portugal to have, at the beginning of the fifteenth century, an able, enterprising sovereign and a considerable number of brave and energetic soldiers, well seasoned in expelling the Moors, in domestic factional wars, and in resisting the pretensions of Spain. These were now in danger of being out of employment; and in default of new quarrels, the king turned their energies to exploring the unknown Atlantic seaboard of Africa. Beginning in 1418, they successively doubled Cape Non, discovered Madeira, passed Cape Bojador, occupied the

Azores, and reached the Senegal and the Cape Verde Islands. Here they paused for a time to take fresh breath. In 1484 they pushed on to the Congo, turned their backs to the sun, and saw the Southern Cross rise in the heavens before them. In 1486 Bartholomew Diaz sighted the Cape of Good Hope; and eleven years later Vasco da Gama rounded that promontory and steered northward toward India.

The Portuguese were as prudent as they were adventurous. They early foresaw the possibility of arriving at vast and rich countries inhabited by people who were not Christians, and who, in consequence, could have no rights even in the land of their birth. It was easy to deal with them, but not so easy to keep other Christian nations from trespassing on the newly discovered regions. Yet it was deemed necessary to have the sole and absolute ownership of all pagan lands reached, regardless of their present occupants, and a bull was therefore obtained from Pope Eugenius IV., granting to Portugal the desired right to all countries discovered or to be discovered, from Cape Non to India. The inducement professedly held out to His Holiness was the great glory that would inure to Christ and his Church from the conversion of these various peoples. There may be differences of opinion how far either party was candid and frank as to his motives; but we can scarcely doubt that the Sovereign Pontiff felt flattered by being thus publicly appealed to as " the disposer of all the crowns of the universe," and that the King of Portugal was more than flattered by the sudden acquisition of regions so vast that his native kingdom was but a speck in comparison. It is true that here and there, in the cooler parts of Europe, men were beginning to appear who might be disposed to question the Pope's right to bestow upon whomsoever he would kingdoms and continents of which he did not know the names or the existence: but such captious persons were few, and supposed to be unimportant; and these geographical exercises of the Holy See continued for a century or two to play an important part in European politics.

While the Portuguese were thus groping their way along the shore eastward toward India, as a blind man guides his steps by the aid of a wall, Columbus conceived the idea of sailing out westward on the wide waste of waters, and thus, as it were, going forth to meet the advance guards of the Mikado and the Great Khan. It would be out of place here to attempt any account of the labors, the disappointments and achievements of Columbus. The moderate space of a few pages would only suffice to tell less than everyone knows already; and to give any adequate account would be to convert the present work into a biography of the discoverer instead of a description of one of the places discovered. Suffice it to say that on Friday, the 3d day of August, 1492, Columbus set sail from Palos with 90 men on board of three little crazy barks, two of which were no better than modern fishing smacks, and that he saw the first land of the western hemisphere on the 12th of October. The land thus seen was one of the Bahama islands, then called by the natives Guanahaní, christened by Columbus as San Salvador, and now known to seafaring men as Cat Island.

It was during this first voyage that Columbus discovered Cuba, which he declared to be " the goodliest land that eye ever saw." From its great extent he believed it to be the extremity of the continent of Asia; and he lived and died in that belief. During his second voyage he made a serious attempt to test the truth of his conjecture. After rounding Cape Maisí he traced the south coast until he had passed the Isle of Pines and was almost within sight of Cape San Antonio, when, seeing no prospect of a termination, he took an oath of every man and boy in the fleet of their belief as to where they were. They all signed a statement that they believed themselves on the coast of Asia. This curious document was in existence in the time of Washington Irving, and it is not likely that it has been destroyed since.

This was one of the least of the many delusions—then common to all the world —under which the Spaniards discovered, colonized, and held their American possessions. A far more serious error, though of a different nature, was their eagerness for certain commodities that contribute to the ostentation and self-indulgence of the rich and the idle rather than to the comfort and sustenance of mankind in general. The chief of these—far excelling all other terrestrial products in importance—was gold; then followed silver, precious stones, pearls, spices, and perfumes. Perhaps there were few in that age capable of understanding that if gold and iron were equally abundant and easily obtained, the gold would be much the less valuable of the two; or that a few pairs of domestic animals and a handful of seeds would be a more precious gift to a new continent than turning all its rocks into gold, and its bowlders and cobblestones into rubies and diamonds. The explorers, like little children at a fair, were attracted by the merest trifles. They scrutinized more carefully the oyster shells thrown up by the waves, suggesting a possibility of pearls, than the richness of the soil and the exuberance of the tropical forests. Wherever they landed, as soon as they could make themselves understood, they inquired for gold. The answers received in Cuba were not encouraging, and seemed to point to another large island that has variously borne the names of Hayti (or Haiti), Hispaniola, and Santo Domingo. This island and its inhabitants presented prospects so inviting that it became the seat of the first Spanish settlement in the New World.

Of the aborigines of Haití, who did not differ from those of Cuba, Columbus thus wrote to their Catholic Majesties:

The king having been informed of our misfortune expressed great grief for our loss, and immediately sent aboard all the people in the place in many large canoes; we soon unloaded the ship of everything that was upon deck, as the king gave us great assistance; he, himself, with his brothers and relations, took all possible care that everything should be properly done, both aboard and on shore. And, from time to time, he sent some of his relations weeping, to beg of me not to be dejected, for he would give me all that he had. I can assure Your Highnesses, that so much care would not have been taken in securing our effects in any part of Spain, as all our property was put together in one place near his palace, until the houses which he wanted to prepare for the custody of it were emptied. He immediately placed a guard of armed men, who watched during the whole night, and those on shore lamented as if they had been much interested in our loss. The people are so affectionate, so tractable, and so peaceable that I swear to Your Highnesses that there is not a better race of men,. nor a better country in the world. They love their neighbor as themselves; their conversation is the sweetest and mildest in the world, cheerful and always accompanied with a smile. And although it is true that they go naked, yet Your Highnesses may be assured that they have many very commendable customs; the king is served with great state, and his behavior is so decent that it is pleasant to see him, as it is likewise the wonderful memory which these people have, and their desire of knowing everything, which leads them to inquire into its causes and effects. *

As there was danger that the Spanish discoveries might come in conflict with those of the Portuguese, Pope Alexander VI., himself of Spanish birth, not only confirmed the right of the Spanish crown to the newly discovered countries, but designated a line to be drawn due north and south, 100 leagues west of the Azores, from one extremity of the world to the other. All pagan lands east of this line were confirmed to Portugal; all to the westward were to be the exclusive property of Spain. No other country could have any share; and a hostile meeting of the two waves of occupancy at the antipodes seems not to have been anticipated.

The Spaniards made their first settlement on the island of Haiti, or Hispaniola. But in eighteen years it was thought to be pretty nearly exhausted. The native population, variously estimated at from one to three million, was reduced to some 50,000 by the hardships of slavery for which they were

* "Life of Christopher Columbus," by his son Don Ferdinand ; chap. xxxii ; vol. ii. of "Churchill's Collection of Voyages," 3d. ed., London, 1744.

physically and mentally unfit. Hence in 1511 Don Diego Columbus, son of the great discoverer, determined to take possession of Cuba. He selected for the enterprise Diego Velásquez, one of his father's companions, whom he sent with a small body of 300 men. They landed at Baracoa without any effective resistance from the feeble and guileless Indians. One native chief named Hatuey, a refugee from Hispaniola, who knew what Spaniards were, attempted opposition; but his followers were soon broken and dispersed, and he himself taken prisoner. Instead of being treated as an honorable captive, he was condemned to be burned alive as a fugitive slave. Then was enacted one of the most horrid of mockeries. When the chief was tied to the stake, and the fagots were piled around him, a Franciscan friar stood by the pile and urged him to abjure the feeble gods of his ancestors and accept Christianity, in order that the same flames which consumed his body might waft his soul to the regions of eternal bliss. Aware that his conversion would not prevent his cremation, he inquired if there were any Spaniards in those happy abodes, and, on being answered

in the affirmative, " I will not go," he said,
" to a place where I may meet one of that
accursed race."*   So great was the terror in-
spired in the natives that there was no further
resistance, and Velásquez, without the loss of
a man, took possession of a country nearly
as large as Pennsylvania. This was the first
pressure of the mailed hand that has now
been laid for nearly four centuries upon the
beautiful island.

The first permanent settlement was at
Santiago de Cuba, a circumstance which gave
priority of rank to the bishop of that diocese,
and eventually led to his elevation to the rank
of archbishop. Within a year or two a footing was also gained at Trinidad and near the
present city of Habana. Thus secured, Cuba
was not considered as of much importance
in itself, but as an intermediate station for
prosecuting enterprises against the mainland.
From that time until near the close of the
eighteenth century she scarcely had a separate
history, and was affected by current events
only in the same manner as the other Antilles
and the adjacent continent.

* Fr. Bartolomé de las Casas, " Brevísima relación de la
destrucción de las Indias."

CHAPTER II.

THE general objects of planting colonies
have been twofold: to open a safety valve for
the outlet of redundant or discontented
population; and to provide closed markets in
which the mother country, and no one else,
might buy cheap and sell dear, and to and
from which she should hold a monopoly of
the carrying trade.

In this respect Spain was not peculiar. It
was the generally understood policy of all
nations; and Spain's misfortune has been her
small capacity to learn or forget. She retains the ideas of the distant past, and cannot
or will not acquire those of the progressive
present. England was once almost as exclusive; but has learned better. The celebrated Navigation Act (12th Charles II.,
chap. xviii.) was to the effect above stated;
and by a later Act (15th Charles II., chap. vii.)
Scotland and Ireland were excluded from the
benefits of the colonial trade. No European

products were to be admitted into the
British colonial plantations except in Eng-
lish-built vessels, manned by Englishmen and
loaded in the ports of England or Wales, or
the town of Berwick-upon-Tweed. Perhaps
England never pretended to restrict the navigation of the high seas; but Spain, by the line
of Pope Alexander, owned the greater part of
the Atlantic, and stories are told of atrocities
committed upon navigators—especially English—caught near its western confines.

When more liberal views were beginning
to prevail in other parts of the world, and
Cromwell proposed that Spain should abol-
ish the Inquisition and admit the free navigation of the western seas, the Spanish
ambassador told him that for his master to
relinquish those prerogatives would be to
give up his two eyes.*

This policy was illustrated by an incident
which took place on the coast of Florida. A
party of French Huguenots settled near the
mouth of the river St. John in 1564. Shortly
after that Avilés de Menéndez, sailing under
orders to " gibbet and behead all Protestants

* Bryan Edwards, "History of the West Indies," vol. i.
p. 191.

in those regions," surprised and massacred those found in the settlement. A party of the French, who were absent at the time, afterward fell into the hands of Avilés, who hanged them all and set up a superscription: "Not as Frenchmen, but as heretics." Retribution, however, fell on the Spaniards, who undertook in the following year to found St. Augustine; for in 1567 a French expeditionary force surprised the settlers, and hanged them, "Not as Spaniards, but as murderers." *

Still intrusions continued, though many intruders were put to death by the Spaniards and many were sent to labor for life in the Mexican mines. In 1650 the Spanish forces attacked the Dutch and English settlements on the island of Santa Cruz and massacred every man, woman, and child; and such acts were continued at intervals far into the eighteenth century.

It was as late as 1738 or 1739 that the incident occurred which gave rise to what Mr. Carlyle has called "The War of Jenkins' Ear." While the English persisted in maintaining a trade in contravention of the Span-

* " Encyclopædia Britannica," ix. 340.

ish restrictions, Captain Jenkins, commanding an English trading ship in the waters of
the Spanish Main, was seized by a Spanish
cruiser. His vessel was searched and he himself, as he testified, subjected to torture. The
Spanish were so irritated at finding little to
convict him of even a technical offense, that,
in foolish bravado, they cut off one of his ears
and told him to take that home and show it
to his king. The captain placed his ear in a
bottle of spirits; and in due time he and it
were presented in the course of a debate in
the House of Commons.* We are of the
same blood, and can imagine the sensation
produced. The result was that Walpole, de-
spite his generally pacific inclination, was
compelled by public sentiment to declare war.

It was indeed impossible for Spain to
maintain her monopoly of the Western hemisphere as against the rest of Europe. Her
pretensions were disregarded or resisted,
especially by the Portuguese, the French, the
English, and the Dutch. In the ever-recur-
ring conflicts from the sixteenth century to
the nineteenth there were many reprisals and

* Bryan Edwards, "History of the West Indies," vol. i.
p. 185.

not a few acts of barbarity, in all of which Cuba was exposed to the common fate.

In 1538 the young city of Habana was laid in ashes by a French privateer. To prevent the recurrence of such a disaster, the governor—the celebrated Fernando de Soto—erected the Castillo de la Fuerza to defend the entrance to the harbor. But the precaution was insufficient, for in 1554 the French again took and destroyed Habana. Two other fortresses were then added, the Punta and the Morro. In January, 1762, near the close of what is known as the Seven Years' War, hostilities were declared against Spain, and during the summer Lord Albemarle, with a fleet of 200 sail in all, and a land force of 14,041 men, attacked Habana. The defense, made by an army of 27,610, was most obstinate, and lasted two months. In a series of brilliant successes, the conquest of Canada and the capture of Habana—victories within a few years over France and Spain—made a vivid impression on the popular mind of Britain. Burns has commemorated the two events in "The Jolly Beggars" by a few spirited lines in which the old soldier sings:

My 'prenticeship I passed where my leader breathed his last,
   When the bloody die was cast on the heights of Abram; .
I served out my trade when the gallant game was played,
   And the Morro low was laid at the sound of the drum.

The British troops held Habana and the surrounding country from August, 1763, until the following year. During their occupation they instituted effective hygienic regulations in the city, and made the port free to the commerce of the world—a change so radical and far-reaching that the Spaniards, upon regaining possession, found it impracticable to re-establish the former restrictive policy.

By the treaty of Paris (February 10, 1763) a large part of the seven years' conquests were restored, among them Habana. England was largely the gainer, receiving from France all the territory claimed by that country east of the Mississippi, together with the islands of Prince Edward, Cape Breton, Dominica, St. Vincent, Tobago, and Minorca. Florida was ceded to England by Spain, which in turn received Louisiana from France. Martinique, Guadeloupe, Pondicherry, and Goree were restored to France.

Those troubled centuries of rival European

rule in the New World gave opportunity for the rise of a body of men—one might almost say an institution—known as the buccaneers. They were smugglers at first, gradually developing into privateers, or even pirates, and were for the most part natives of France, England, and Holland—the rivals of Spain. They differed from full-grown pirates in that they did not prey upon mankind generally, but preferably, if not exclusively, upon Spaniards. Hence it was not generally to the interest of other powers to discourage them. After the heedless tyranny of the discoverers had destroyed the native population of Haití, immense herds of wild cattle came to range over the uninhabited parts of the interior. The natives had learned a method of preserving the flesh of these animals by drying and smoking, and they used a word *bucan* to designate the kiln or structure for conducting the process. Europeans, venturing into those seas, not only procured supplies of this food, but developed an illicit trade—as all trade was illicit—of carrying *buccanned* beef to other places; and both the preparers and the carriers acquired a name which is generally written " buccaneer " (Span. *bucanero*).

As the seafaring buccaneers were liable to seizure everywhere by the Spaniards, they had to be prepared for defense, and so acquired a warlike character. They also found it to their interest to make common cause against a common enemy. Thus combined, they became not only formidable to Spain but an ally worth conciliating by her enemies; and with English and French assistance, they undertook, in 1625, to establish a permanent settlement in the island of St. Christopher (or St. Kitts). About five years later they set up a depot on one of the Bahamas. Besides being independent rovers, they formed a mercenary navy, at the service of any power at war with Spain, and, receiving letters of marque and reprisal as privateers, became entitled to the rights of belligerents.

After the British conquest of Jamaica in 1655, that island, which they had helped to gain, became the center of their power, whence they issued, no longer merely to intercept the dwindling commerce of Spain, and seize her returning treasure ships, but to plunder the cities of Cuba and of the mainland.

These depredations continued long after

the treaty of 1670, between England and
Spain, proclaimed peace in the West Indian
colonies. In 1671 Henry Morgan, a Welshman, and chief of the floating republic, set
sail for a convenient port in the Caribbean
with 39 ships and 2000 men, crossed the isthmus, and plundered Panamá. After his return he became Sir Henry Morgan, by the
grace of King Charles, and deputy governor
of Jamaica. In 1680 John Coxon, with 300
men, landed on the coast of Darién and
plunged into the wilderness with only what
they could carry on their backs. Their steps
were directed by the Indians, whose hostility to the Spaniards was as great as their
own, and much more justifiable. On reaching one of the short rivers that empty
into the South Sea, they descended it in a
fleet of canoes and paralyzed resistance by
their sudden and wild appearance and the
terror of their name. They were able to surprise and seize four armed vessels, and then
success flowed in upon them like the tide.
Recruits crossed the isthmus and joined
them; and they ravaged the islands and coast
towns from California to Peru. By a supreme effort, in 1685, a fleet of fourteen sail

was gotten together and confronted the invaders in the Bay of Panamá, but did not dare to attack. From that time, however, combined opposition from without, and vices and dissensions within, made their decline even more rapid than their rise, and now for nearly two centuries the buccaneers have been but a memory and a name.

Up to the close of the eighteenth century the people of Cuba, few in number, lived a retired rustic life. Their magnificent harbors were closed against the commerce of the world and could be entered only by stealth or force. Spain was not in a condition to be a large purchaser for the special products of the island. The greater part of the annual product of the soil was consumed on the *haciendas* or farms on which it grew. Theirs was the undeveloped state in which the rudiments of every trade are to be found in every neighborhood, and on every large estate. Education, as now understood, was almost wholly wanting; and the little that was called for was chiefly possessed by ecclesiastics from the parent country. Gold and silver had not been discovered in remunerative quantities; and, as stated above, the most obvious use of the island was as a midway station to facilitate enterprises against the mainland. The principles of public wealth were not better or more universally understood at the close of the fifteenth than at the end of the nineteenth century. Spain was willing to repeat the experience of Midas, turn everything she touched into a metal for coinage, and perish of hunger in the midst of imaginary affluence.* It was at the old capital of Santiago de Cuba that the expedition of Cortes was fitted out to subjugate the golden realms of Montezuma; and it was from Cuba that the romantic adventurer, Fernando de Soto, set out on his four years of weary wandering, to seek the fountain of eternal youth and find a grave beneath the waters of the Mississippi.

* See Appendix A.

CHAPTER III.

From the restoration of Cuba to Spain by the peace of 1763 until the close of the century, there followed a period of unwonted prosperity, varying with the character of the successive governors. Of these Luis de las Casas, appointed in 1790, was one of the most able and progressive, as was shown by his success in restraining the negro population under the excitement attending the revolution in Santo Domingo, and by the new impulse which he imparted to the agriculture and commerce of the island. It was under his guidance that trade with the North American republic began to assume importance, and to his efforts was due the transfer of the remains of Columbus from Santo Domingo to their present resting place in the cathedral at Habana.

De las Casas was succeeded, in December, 1796, by the Count of Santa Clara, who took an ardent interest in the welfare of Cuba, and notably in its military defenses.   Most of the present fortifications on the island were originated by him, and the Batería de Santa Clara, outside of Habana, was named in his honor.

During the years from 1726 to 1796, a great navy yard grew up on the Bay of Habana, and 114 war vessels were built there to convoy the Spanish treasure ships.   But they were closed, at the date last named, on the demand of the ship-builders of Spain that the work should be done in the mother country.   This was one of the earliest causes of an ill feeling between the islanders and the inhabitants of the peninsula.

It was toward the close of the eighteenth century that sugar became an important article of general commerce.   But it was not even then an article of common consumption, and one of the earliest prices noted is equivalent to 43 cents a pound, at a time when the purchasing power of money was at least twice as great as it is now.   The consumption of sugar in the United Kingdom is at present about 70 times as great as it was a century ago, and has been coincident with the increased use of tea and coffee.

When the Spanish Bourbons were deposed by Napoleon in 1808 every member of the provincial council of Cuba took an oath to preserve the island for their legitimate sovereign, thus earning for their country the title of " The Ever-faithful Isle." This fidelity was followed, if not rewarded, by a line of captains general continuing till the present time, varying in individual character, but all invested with the powers of Oriental despotism, or of the commander of a ship at sea. Their functions were defined by a royal decree of May 28, 1825, of which the following is a translation:

His Majesty, the King, our Lord, desiring to obviate the inconveniences that might, in extraordinary cases, result from a division of command, and from the interferences and prerogatives of the respective officers: for the important end of preserving in that precious island his legitimate sovereign authority and the public tranquillity, through proper means, has resolved, in accordance with the opinion of his council of ministers, to give to your Excellency the fullest authority, bestowing upon you all the powers which by the royal ordinances are granted to the governors of besieged cities. In consequence of this His Majesty gives to your Excellency the most ample and unbounded power, not only to send away from the island any persons in office, whatever their occupation, rank, class, or condition, whose continuance therein your Excellency may deem injurious, or whose conduct, public or private, may alarm you, replacing them with persons faithful to His Majesty, and deserving of all the confidence of your Excellency ; but also to suspend the execution of any order whatsoever, or any general provision made concerning any branch of the administration as your Excellency may think most suitable to the royal service.

This decree is still substantially the supreme law of Cuba. Its originating cause lay outside of the island. Revolutionary movements had begun in Spanish America in 1810, and after 14 years of guerrilla warfare European power had practically ceased from the Canadian lakes to Cape Horn. In 1821 Santo Domingo declared its independence of Spain; and in the same year Florida came into the possession of the United States, many of its people crossing over to Cuba. These events could not fail to infuse into the islanders a leaven of unrest; and the severe repressive measures adopted have thus far yielded no happy results. While Canada, under a mild and all but nominal sovereignty, is as peaceful and loyal as Devonshire or Scotland, Cuba, under martial law, is kept in a state of chronic insurrection. More exasperating even than severe laws has been the practice, continued to the present time, of billeting upon the resources of the island, first, loyalist refugees from Spanish America, and, afterward, swarms of the retainers of Spanish politicians.

Secret political societies of malcontents began to spring up in Cuba. The two elements of the population—the advocates of a liberal constitution and the partisans of a rigid colonial control—were gathering in opposing factions. An attempt at open revolt was made so early as 1823 by the association known as the " Soles de Bolívar," but it was frustrated before reaching maturity, and the leaders who did not escape from the island were arrested and punished.

In 1826 Cuban refugees in Mexico and Colombia planned and even began to organize an invasion of Cuba to be led by the great liberator, Simón Bolívar; but their scheme came to nought for lack of adequate support. Later (1827--29) they organized a secret society denominated the " Black Eagle," for the purpose of forming a second invading expedition. This society had its headquarters in Mexico, and established recruiting agencies and branch offices in the United States and in many towns in Cuba, but the determined opposition of the slave-holding interests of both countries rendered this otherwise promising conspiracy abortive from the very outset; and the ringleaders were caught by the Spanish authorities.

A much more serious matter was the insurrection, or anticipated insurrection, in 1844, of the slaves on the sugar plantations about Matanzas. It was largely a matter of suspicion; and the difficulty of obtaining sufficient evidence was so great that witnesses were examined under torture. By such means 1346 persons were convicted, of whom 78 were shot and the others subjected to various degrees of minor punishment. Of those adjudged guilty 14 were white, 1242 free colored persons, and 59 slaves.

A few years later Narciso López, a native of Venezuela who had served in the Spanish army and had risen to the rank of major general, started a revolutionary movement in the center of the island. Being unsuccessful, he made his escape, together with a number of Cubans, to this country and established in New York a center for that sympathy which has been so often and so strongly aroused in behalf of Cuba. In 1848 President Polk made overtures to the Spanish Government with a view to purchasing the island for $100,000,000. About that time the people of the slave States were filled with apprehensions in view of the growing population, wealth, congressional representation, and anti-slavery feeling of the North and West; and there was a strong sentiment in favor of annexing Cuba and dividing it into as many slave States as possible; the chief if not the sole, inducement being additional votes in Congress. The warm-blooded youth of the South were filled with filibustering dreams, as the chivalry of the Middle Ages had been roused by the preaching of successive crusades.

In 1849 López made an attempt to return to Cuba with a small party, but was intercepted by the authorities of the United States. The following year, however, he organized outside of our jurisdiction and succeeded in reaching the island with a force of 600 men. He effected a landing at Cárdenas, but was immediately compelled to re-embark, and was chased by a Spanish ship of war to Key West, where his party was disbanded.

Encouraged by some revolutionary manifestations in Cuba, López hastened from New Orleans in 1851, with 450 men on board the steamer *Pampero*. He landed at Playitas, 30 miles from Habana, but was speedily confronted by a force greatly superior to his own in numbers, equipment, and training. Crittenden of Kentucky, second in command, was left with 130 men to bring up the supplies, while López, with the main body, pushed forward into the interior. Thus separated, both were surrounded. Crittenden's party, when reduced to 50 men, were captured and shot. The sufferings of López and his men were severe and prolonged. When no longer able to fight, they wandered in the dense woods without food, shoes, or shelter, until the last were captured. López was executed, but the remnant of his band were released.

In the spring of 1850 occurred one of the earliest of those incidents which have done so much to produce public irritation in this country. It was the case of the *Black Warrior*, a steamer òwned in New York, and plying regularly between that city and Mobile, and making the round trip, as nearly as might be, within the calendar month. She was the largest steamer in the coasting trade, had accommodations for 200 cabin passengers, and, when arrested, had on board 960 bales of cotton. In going and returning she touched at Habana to deliver and receive mail and passengers, but not to discharge or take on board any freight. In strict accordance with the customs laws, which were very stringent, she should have exhibited each time a manifest of her cargo. But that could answer no useful purpose, as none of it was to be moved. So she was entered and cleared as " in ballast," to save time and trouble; having been so entered and cleared 36 times in succession, with the full knowledge and consent of the revenue officers, and of all who cared to know, and in accordance with a written general order of the Cuban authorities, dated April 27, 1847. On the 28th of February, 1850, the steamer was stopped in the harbor of Habana for having an undeclared cargo on board, and was not permitted to leave the port. The cargo was confiscated and taken on shore, and a fine of twice its value declared against the captain and vessel. Captain Bullock refused to pay any fine and protested against the whole proceeding as violent, wrongful, and in bad ·faith. The officials had sought to induce him to lend color to their acts by opening the hatches and getting the hoisting tackle in place, but he had steadily refused; and when they performed these acts themselves, he declared it a forcible seizure, hauled down his colors, and, taking them with him, left the vessel as a Spanish capture. He and his crew and passengers made their way to the United States as best they could. The owners of the steamer then preferred a claim for $300,000 indemnity, which was paid after a delay of five years.

The case of the *Black Warrior* was one of the incidents that led to the celebrated Ostend Conference.

In 1852 the governments of Great Britain and France submitted to that of the United States a draft of a tripartite convention, by which each should be bound not to acquire Cuba or suffer any other power to do so. The proposal was, after consideration, declined, on the triple ground of (*a*) avoiding " entangling alliances," (*b*) that it would be unwise, if not unconstitutional, to tie our hands for the future, regardless of contingencies, and (*c*) that, on geographical grounds, while England and France were making very slight concessions, we were asked to make a very important one.

In 1854 preparations were made in Cuba and in the United States for another attempt at revolution, to be conducted by General Quitman of Mississippi; but in the following spring the leaders were betrayed and executed, and the enterprise came to nothing.

The Ostend Manifesto (1854) signed by Mr. Buchanan, Mr. Mason, and Mr. Soulé, strongly recommended the purchase of Cuba for $120,000,000, and that in no event should it be allowed to come under the power of any other European government than the one by which it was then held.

The next 14 years was a period of comparative quiet and prosperity. During that time, in 1858, the subject of the acquisition of Cuba was discussed in the Senate of the United States, but no action was taken.

A revolution broke out in Spain in 1868, and on September 30 Queen Isabella left the country, never to return. On the 8th of October a provisional ministry was formed;

and two days later a declaration of Cuban independence was issued at Manzanillo. This was the first step in what has thus far been the most protracted and successful attempt at revolution in the island. High hopes were entertained of effective aid from the United States; but public attention in this country was then absorbed by the problems of reconstruction, and the expectations were disappointed.

CHAPTER IV.

It seems necessary here to pause and seek for some permanent and effective cause for these repeated risings. Any charges of wanton cruelty on the part of Spain, or allegations that the rebels are only a negro rabble, are alike unfounded. Spain, like the other countries around the Mediterranean, is old, exhausted, and poor. In her running account of centuries she has reached a point where the balance against her is a debt out of all proportion to her resources—a debt that can never be paid. To pay the interest necessitates the most grinding oppression. The moving impulse is not malice, but the greed of the famishing; and oppressor and oppressed are alike objects for sympathy. Spain, although poor, has a voice in her own affairs; Cuba is naturally the richest spot in the child-king's dominions, and cannot protect itself. When more revenue is raised than is expended in the island, the excess, under the euphonious name of *sobrante*, or surplus, goes into the royal exchequer; and it is indispensable that there should be a pretty good *sobrante*.

The annual revenue raised in the island in 1868 approximated $26,000,000, and preparations were in progress for largely increasing the exactions. Indeed the causes of these repeated rebellions have been largely financial. Captain General Dulce, in writing to the minister for the colonies in 1867, said:

The cause of trouble and of the inquietude which appears in the island of Cuba should be sought for to a great extent in the tariff laws, which, under pretext of protection, make impossible a commerce carried on in good faith. . . The customhouse system is very expensive, overloaded with formalities which do not prevent fraud, but which embarrass and annoy honest trade. The ordinance of *matrículas*, instead of protecting industry upon the seas, has well-nigh destroyed it.

One of the Cuban deputies to the Cortes said, in a speech delivered in 1866:

I foresee a catastrophe near at hand, in case Spain persists in remaining deaf to the just reclamations of the Cubans. Look at the old colonies of the American Continent. All have ended in conquering their independence.

Let Spain not forget the lesson: let the Government be just to the colonies that remain. Thus she will consolidate her dominion over people who only aspire to be good sons of a worthy mother, but who are not willing to live as slaves under the scepter of a tyrant.

The large revenue raised was not employed judiciously or economically. The captain general received an annual salary of $50,000 at a time when the President of the United States was getting half that amount. The governor of each province had $12,000, while the prime minister of Spain had to be content with $6000. The salaries of the archbishop of Santiago de Cuba and the bishop of Habana were each $18,000. Incident to all offices, civil and ecclesiastical, from the highest to the lowest, were what Americans call "perquisites," and sometimes by a term still broader, which might amount to as much as the nominal salary. The manner of obtaining these was infinitely varied, but a single instance, applicable to the tax on incomes, will give a general idea of their nature. A planter makes up and hands in his return, putting his income for the year at $10,000. The collector expresses great dissatisfaction, insisting that it ought to be

$15,000. After a due amount of argument the planter proposes to split the difference. Then the collector, with effusive politeness and many assurances of his anxiety to be obliging, consents to the compromise. The tax on the difference—the $2500—is paid on the spot and goes into the collector's pocket, and the original $10,000 remains on the tax-book. This wholesale corruption was universal and universally known. The peculation in the customhouse at Habana was estimated at 40 per cent. and at Santiago de Cuba 70 per cent. of the entire receipts.

There was yet another grievance, if it were not merely another aspect of the same. All offices in Church and state, except the lowest in remote districts, were filled by persons sent from Spain. The Spanish statesman, in addition to providing places for his own family, discharged his political obligations by obtaining for his friends and adherents situations as rich as he was able to command. The official went to the island as a foreign master, with little sympathy for its people, to whom he was in no way amenable. He came to fill an empty purse, to return some day and excite the envy of Spanish grandees by the splendor of his equipage, and aid the popular delusion that the impoverished isle was an inexhaustible mine of wealth.

The marked partiality thus shown for persons of European birth produced a jealous and bitter feeling between the *insulares* and the *peninsulares*, as the two parties were called, and, as a rule, in the revolts of the past fifty years a distinct line has been drawn between these islanders and the continentals. Out of this distinction grew the military and political organization of the latter known as the Cuban Volunteers (*Instituto de los Voluntarios de Cuba*), which has been an important factor in the affairs of the island. Bodies of volunteers had indeed appeared at various times from an early period in the history of Cuba, and they gained especial distinction during the British attack in 1762; but the present corps dates its legal existence and formal organization from the royal decree of July 7, 1872, at which time it numbered 80,000 men. They are analogous to the National Guard of the United States; are without pay, except when called into active service; provide their own clothing; but are furnished with arms, ammunition, and armories at the public expense. Their chief duties are to guard towns and public property and suppress disorders, but, though seldom called upon for actual fighting, they are liable to be summoned by their commander, the captain general, to serve in any part of the island. They are so far favored that nominal service in this corps is accepted in part in place of actual military service under draft, so that one may escape two-thirds of the period of conscript service by becoming enrolled among the volunteers. Most of them are active politicians; and by their peninsular connections and their true blue Spanish loyalty they wield a powerful influence, often controlling or displacing even the governor general.*

By means of differential duties, Spain had still almost a monopoly of the trade to Cuba, while making the Cubans pay high for all that they received from the mother country. Flour was burdened with duties so heavy that wheaten bread ceased to be an article of com-

---

* In June, 1870, they took it upon themselves to arrest, and send back to Spain, Captain General Dulce, with whom they were dissatisfied. They deposed the governor of the province of Matanzas, General López Pinto, for like reasons.

mon food with the bulk of the people. The annual consumption of bread in Spain was 400 pounds per capita, while in Cuba it was 53 pounds 9 ounces. At that time a barrel of flour could be bought in New York, carried to some port in Spain, whereby it became naturalized as Spanish flour, reshipped across the Atlantic and delivered in Habana for $8.75; while, if sent direct from an American port, it would have cost the wholesale dealer $10.46.*

Among the curiosities of Cuban finance was the following postal regulation: A letter from Europe, although prepaid, was charged 25 cents at the Cuban post office, and even then was not carried to its destination. For delivery there was an additional charge; so a Cuban, receiving a prepaid letter at his own door, had to pay 37½ cents additional postage. Books and parcels were similarly treated.

Imposts for revenue alone may be so heavy as to defeat their own object. The duties laid on Cuban products in Spanish ports

* Under a convention which went into effect July 1, 1892, the duties on flour and many other American products were greatly reduced ; but the United States tariff legislation of 1894 had the effect of restoring the former rates.

made them too costly for the Spanish people. The small quantity of sugar produced in the peninsula was aided by a bounty; that of Cuba was taxed on both sides of the Atlantic till finally supplanted by German beet sugar.   Of the tobacco imported into Spain at the time referred to (1868), 70 per cent. was from foreign countries; thus presenting the strange spectacle of a nation procuring from abroad articles which her own colonies were above all fitted to produce.

Between 1860 and 1870 Spain was engaged in wars with Morocco, Santo Domingo, Mexico, Chile, Peru, and Cochin China, in addition to disturbances and revolution at home.   The condition of things was desperate, the pressure of debt insupportable. Great additions were made to the demands on Cuba.   It was shown by a committee of the Cortes that the increase in two years, 1865--66 and 1866--67, was $14,780,150.   The revenue of the island had been, in 1857, $17,960,000; it was now proposed to raise in 1867--68 over $40,000,000; but the whole was never collected.   The condition was deplorable.   While the people of Spain were paying $3.23 per capita of interest on the national debt, the Cubans, who had had no part or interest in contracting that debt, were paying $6.39. The cities were hopelessly in debt, unable to meet the most necessary municipal expenses, or provide proper sewerage, garbage service, and street cleaning, so essential in that climate. It was even asserted that the municipal gas bills were eighteen months in arrears in Santiago de Cuba, the city where the customs revenues were chiefly absorbed by peculation. Schools were closed and teachers unemployed for want of funds. There was but one asylum in the island for the insane—that in Habana; and in other places these unfortunate beings were confined in the unsanitary cells of the common jails. To crown all, amid " poverty, sickness, and dirt," in a country a great part of whose surface was still a virgin forest, church and state holidays, added to the Sabbaths of the world, exempted one-third of the year from industrial occupations.

There was at that time an active abolition party in Cuba—not philanthropic dreamers, but economists who computed that slavery was an unprofitable form of labor. Their views were moderate. They proposed that the owner should be paid $450 for each slave between the ages of 7 and 60 years, and that this should be paid by the island without affecting Spain in any way. The Cuban delegates pressed this plan before the Cortes until action was taken in 1870.

The foregoing were the principal causes which led to the attempt at revolution in 1868. And a great part of them still remain.

CHAPTER V.

SEVERAL months before the revolution in Spain and the abdication of Isabella, measures had been secretly concerted in Cuba for an attempt to achieve independence. But matters were progressing so rapidly in the mother country that, on October 10, 1868, Carlos M. de Céspedes, a lawyer of Bayamo, took the initiative with 128 ill-armed men and issued a declaration of independence at Yara. This declaration justified itself by referring in the following terms to the grievances above stated:

And as Spain has many a time promised us Cubans to respect our rights, without having hitherto fulfilled her promises; as she continues to tax us heavily, and by so doing is likely to destroy our wealth; as we are in danger of losing our property, our lives, and our honor under further Spanish dominion, etc., etc.

Within a few weeks Céspedes was at the head of 15,000 men, poorly armed and equipped, but resolute. In no long time a constitution was drawn up, providing ior a republican form of government, an elective president and vice president, a cabinet, and a single legislative chamber. It also declared the immediate abolition of slavery. This constitution was promulgated at Guaimaro, in Central Cuba, on the 10th of April, 1869. The legislature, whose election could not have been very regular, met soon after and elected Céspedes president and Francisco M. Aguilero vice president.

For the first two years the revolutionists were generally successful. They were victorious in almost every engagement. Mr. Dupuy de Lome, the representative of Spain near the Government of the United States, says* that the greater and better part of the representative Cubans were in sympathy with the insurrection. But the power of Spain to furnish war material and fresh troops was greater than that of the insurgents. Fresh regiments came over equipped with the best modern arms, while the Cubans were always badly supplied, and depended largely on what they could capture from the royal troops. The coast was patrolled by a Spanish squad-

* In his article in the New York *Herald* of February 23, 1896.

ron, the most effective part of which was a fleet of 30 light-draft gunboats.

In the springtide of their success the Cubans were recognized as belligerents by Chile, Bolivia, Guatemala, the (then) United States of Colombia, and the Mexican Congress. Their independence was acknowledged by Peru on the 13th of June, 1869.

The insurgents kept the field until the spring of 1871, with a force aggregating perhaps 50,000 men. But the majority were without arms; and supplies of all kinds were insufficient and uncertain. It was then that the forces operating in the large district of Camagüey, in Central Cuba, indicated a willingness to lay down their arms if their lives should be spared. The proposition being accepted, they surrendered. General Agramonte, their commander, who refused to yield, was left with no other support than 35 men and his dignity. Around these as a nucleus he organized a body of cavalry, and maintained the war for two years longer, when he was killed in action.

Military operations—chiefly skirmishing— were carried on in 1873 more actively than in any other period of the war, especially in

Eastern Cuba, which, from its mountainous character and distance from the capital, is most capable of maintaining independence.

In the fall of that year the Cuban congress deposed President Céspedes, who, after his retirement, was found and killed by the Spaniards. Salvador Cisneros, the present president of revolutionary Cuba, was elected in his place. He is a scion of the old Spanish nobility, being formerly known as the Marqués de Santa Lucía, and was distinguished by his high social rank, his wealth, and his abilities. In joining the revolution he renounced his title, and his estates were confiscated. A small part was restored to him on the return of peace.

The war dragged on in a desultory way until 1878, with heavy losses and slight gains on either side. On the whole, the revolutionists were slowly losing ground. This was testified by their internal dissensions, if by nothing else. Perhaps no party was ever long or deeply embarrassed without becoming divided. In the mean time Spain kept sending every year fresh levies to the island, only to fall by the diseases of the climate and the hands of bushwhackers. We may pity the brave Spanish youths that were sent so far to a warfare that could yield no laurels, for, as they were considered to be fighting merely a " horde of bandits," their victories could not bring them the same honors, nor their defeats the same compensations, that were allowed to troops in recognized warfare. Our U. S. soldiers who have been engaged in fighting Indians will realize the difference between " dead on the field of battle " and " slain by bandits."

General Martínez de Campos, then in command of the Spanish forces in Cuba, resorted to negotiation. The Cubans listened to his overtures, and after a due amount of preliminaries, terms of peace * were concluded in February, 1878, at the camp of San Antonio, near El Zanjon. Free pardon was offered to all who had taken part in the rebellion, and those who wished to leave the island were to be allowed to do so.

The numbers engaged and the losses on the Cuban side can never be ascertained; but on the part of Spain minima are obtainable. The records of the Cuerpo de Sanidad Militar in the War Office at Madrid show the total

*See Appendix D.

deaths for the ten years to have been, in the regular land forces, 81,098.*   On deducting the losses of the last year—7500—the loss in the previous nine years is found to be 73,598. Add to this the number in the field during the last year, 81,700—in other words, all who had previously died and all who were still alive—and we have a minimum total of 155,-298, to which may be added the 80,000 Volunteers already mentioned, making a total land force of 235,298 at the disposal of the captain general in the course of the war.

* The strength of the forces engaged, and the losses for each year, were as follows :

Year.	Force in the Field.	Deaths.	Year.	Force in the Field.	Deaths.
1869	35,570	5,504	1874	62,578	5,923
1870	47,242	9,395	1875	63,212	6,361
1871	55,357	6,574	1876	78,099	8,482
1872	58,708	7,780	1877	90,245	17,677
1873	52,500	5,902	1878	81,700	7,500

In the year 1877, with an active army of 90,000, there were 15,708 men on the hospital returns.

The percentage of deaths during the entire campaign was as follows:

Killed, and died from wounds,   .   .   .   8½ per cent.
Died from disease, ...   9½   "
                                                Total,   .   .   18   per cent.

CHAPTER VI.

During the ten years' war there were two incidents which merit a somewhat detailed consideration,—the affair of the students and the affair of the *Virginius*,—of which the former shocked humanity and the latter came near precipitating a war with the United States.

Partisan zeal has sometimes betrayed the organization known as the Cuban Volunteers into acts of wanton cruelty. The dead body of one of their number had been placed in a public tomb in Habana, and, later, the repository was found to have been in some manner defaced (by writing on the glass of the door, it has been asserted). Suspicion pointed to the students of the university. On the complaint of the Volunteer Corps, 43 of these young men were arrested and put on trial for the offense. An officer of the regular army from Spain voluntarily defended them, before the military tribunal, with ability and manly warmth; and they were acquitted. The

Volunteers were not satisfied, and obtained from the weakness of the governor general an order for the assembling of a second court martial, of which two-thirds of the members should be Volunteers, thus making that body at once accuser and judge.   By this tribunal the accused were as a matter of course all condemned—eight to be shot, and the others to terms of imprisonment and hard labor.   Next morning (November 27, 1871) 15,000 Volunteers turned out under arms and executed the eight boys.   The affair shot a thrill of horror and indignation through the United States and was censured by the Spanish Cortes; but there was no attempt at punishment.

The *Virginius* was a steamer built in England for use as a blockade-runner during the American Civil War.   Being captured, she was brought to the navy yard at Washington, and there sold at auction to one John F. Patterson, who took her to New York, and made oath that he was a citizen of the United States and sole owner of the vessel.   He obtained registry for her at the customhouse, and all papers necessary for the protection of the ship as a part of the American merchant marine; and she sailed for the port of Curaçoa, in the Dutch West Indies, on the 4th of October, 1870, but without cargo or insurance. It came to light several years later that Patterson was not the *bona fide* owner of the vessel, but that her purchase money was furnished and her movements controlled by a *junta* of Cuban sympathizers. She cruised up and down in the Caribbean sea for three years, occasionally visiting the coast of Cuba, and never voluntarily returned to the waters of the United States.

On the 23d of October, 1873, she was regularly cleared from the port of Kingston, Jamaica, for Puerto Limón, Costa Rica; and, on the morning of the 31st, was seen hovering on the coast of Cuba, was chased by the Spanish cruiser *Tornado* until within sight of Jamaica, captured, and brought into the harbor of Santiago de Cuba on the 1st of November. There were 155 persons on board. The names of far the greater number were Spanish, while 45 indicated Saxon lineage, and it was apparent that some of the others might be citizens of the United States.

As the *Virginius* displayed the American colors and was chartered and cleared as an

American vessel, she had a *prima facie* claim to protection as such until her right should be disproved. Hence Mr. E. G. Schmitt, the American vice consul at Santiago, was prompt and urgent in demanding access to the prisoners with a view to protecting the rights of the vessel and any on board who might be American citizens. He was treated with great discourtesy by the provincial governor, who told him in effect that it was none of his (the consul's) business, and persisted in declaring that they were all pirates and would be dealt with as such. Mr. Schmitt was even refused the use of the marine cable to consult with the consul at Kingston. He would thus have been left entirely helpless but for the friendly aid of the British and French consuls. His next step was to search for, and ask the protection of, a United States war vessel, but that was necessarily a matter of time. Meanwhile the authorities in Jamaica were aroused, and H. M. S. *Niobe*, commanded by Sir Lambton Lorraine, left Kingston on the evening of the 6th of November and reached Santiago on the 8th. The *Virginius* had been brought in about sunset on the 1st, and a court martial to try the prisoners met at nine o'clock next morning. Up to some hour on the 8th, 53 persons had been tried and shot. It has been asserted that Sir Lambton threatened to bombard the town unless the executions were stopped instantly. We have not been able to find that in any of the official documents at hand; yet it is not unlikely that that was one of the points tacitly understood; and that the sanguinary governor was led to contemplate the possibility of having his palace shelled. In any case there was no more shooting. The *Niobe* was re-enforced by the *Woodlark* on the 14th of the month, and Commander Cushing arrived two days later with the U. S. S. *Wyoming*.

It may be interesting at this point to see a sample of the correspondence between the American vice consul and the governor of Santiago de Cuba. Those expressions in the governor's letter which seem intended to be especially pungent or crushing are italicized. On the 4th of November his Excellency wrote:

I have received your communications, one dated the 2d instant and the remaining two others the 3d instant;

the first inquiring if it was true that a telegram had been detained by my orders which you had addressed to the United States consul in Kingston, Jamaica, asking information as to the nationality of the steamer *Virginius*, seized on the high seas as a pirate by the Spanish cruiser *Tornado.* In my desire to correspond duly to the *exquisite zeal* which you show in this matter, I would have replied at once to your communication, but as I received it precisely at the moment of important and peremptory affairs, to which I had to devote myself exclusively ; and, further, as the past two days were holidays, upon which the officials do not come to the offices, *being engaged, as well as everyone else, in meditation of the divine mysteries of All Saints' and the commemoration of All Souls' days, as prescribed by our holy religion ;* it was impossible for me, until early this morning, to comply with your wishes. . .

Neither could I foresee your desire to repair with such haste to the jail where the prisoners were incarcerated, much less that you desired to do so, *showing an officiousness so marked,* when you had received from none of them any remonstrance whatever, which they would have made at once, through my conduct, if their conscience had permitted them to even suppose that they were innocent and worthy of the protection of your vice consulate, *undoubtedly impelled thereto on this occasion for unknown and suspicious purposes.*

.   .   .   .   .

Such conduct, especially after you were advised by the fiscal that Mr. O'Ryan was an Englishman, obliges me to apply to the government, and *propose that your exequatur to perform the duties of your vice consulate be withdrawn,* as an officer who addresses protests so slightly founded, and who, after that, attempts to surprise the intention of the Spanish authorities, accustomed to act with the rectitude and loyalty known to all, *cannot help compromising the honor of the country he represents.*

Mr. Schmitt's position was relatively obscure and his name was not one of national celebrity; hence it is all the more gratifying to see that he could bear himself in act and word so as to maintain his self-respect and reflect honor on his country. In his reply he said:

I should have been the last person to disturb the important duties of your Excellency, and the religious meditations which your Excellency's subordinates were indulging in, had it not been that I considered the case a pressing one, and imagined that, where there was sufficient time to censure and detain my telegram, there might have been also time for a few lines of explanation, with the additional motive of my second dispatch, that I observed that the circumstances which your Excellency enumerates were no hindrance to the dispatch of other business connected with the steamer.

.   .   .   .   .

I shall, therefore, abstain from saying anything further on this point than that it seems to me, considering that the *Virginius* was flying the United States flag at the time of her capture, that she claimed to be a United States merchant-steamer, and her papers as such were surrendered by her captain to the boarding officer of the steamer *Tornado*, it would have been a delicate attention on the part of your Excellency to have informed me thereof and that the use of such flag and papers was an abuse on the goodness of the country which I represent, in order that I might have brought the same to the notice of my Government.

.   .   .   .   .

Finally, I note your Excellency's intention to apply for the revocation of my exequatur, and, while ignorant of any cause given therefor, I can only assure your Excellency that my conscience being perfectly clear in the question, and having acted honorably and as I considered for the best, the result of your Excellency's application is to me a matter of profound indifference.

The charge of piracy was so unfounded that the deplorable results alone saved it from being ridiculous. A pirate is one who, without authority from any government, commits, upon the high seas, depredations that would be felony upon the land. The *Virginius* committed no depredations, and so lacked the first essential of piracy. She was entitled to no protection, as her American papers were obtained under false pretenses; but that was an offense only against the laws and dignity of the United States, and a ship without a country has a natural right peaceably to navigate the high seas unmolested. The *Virginius* was a smuggler and ocean tramp, sailing under false colors, ready to carry any person or thing,—however prohibited in any particular country,—and the evidence showed that she had not always been employed in the interest of the Cubans.

While the above events were in progress the United States was represented at Madrid by General Daniel E. Sickles. On receiving, on the 6th of November, the first intimation of what had taken place, he called at the Ministry of State, and saw the President in the evening. In reporting the result of this interview, he wrote:

President Castelar received these observations with his usual kindness, and told me confidentially that, at seven o'clock in the morning, as soon as he read the telegram from Cuba, and without reference to any international question, for that, indeed had not occurred to him, he at once sent a message to the captain general, admonishing him that the death penalty must not be imposed upon any non-combatant without the previous approval of the Cortes, nor upon any person taken in arms against the Government without the sanction of the executive.

The President's order failed to get farther than Habana in time to do any good. There had been two telegraphic lines between that city and Santiago de Cuba, one around the coast and one overland. The for-

mer had been for some time out of repair;
and it was a curious fact, that might or might
not be significant, that the land line failed the
very day that the *Virginius* was brought in.
It was equally curious that it found a tongue
the day that the *Niobe* came into port.

As no satisfactory answer was received or
could be received, the patience of the Minister of State broke down under the constant
pressure of General Sickles' remonstrances;
and he began to imitate at humble distance
the style of the Cuban governor. The general replied in a manner equally pointed,
but more dignified. It is difficult to refrain
from giving at least one brief specimen from
this diplomatic war of words. General
Sickles was instructed by the Secretary of
State to present a solemn protest against the
barbarities perpetrated at Santiago; and in
performing that duty he repeated, as nearly
as might be, the words dictated from Washington. To this protest the Minister of
State, Señor Carvajal, made an ill-tempered
reply, in the course of which he used the not
very happy expression: "The protest being
thus rejected with *screne energy.*" The
American envoy, after correcting a number

of misconceptions, concluded his rejoinder by saying:

And if at last, under the good auspices of Mr. Carvajal, with the aid of that *serenity* that is unmoved by slaughter and that *energy* that rejects the voice of humanity, which even the humblest may utter and the most powerful cannot hush, this government is successful in restoring order and peace and liberty where hitherto, and now, all is tumult and conflict and despotism, the fame of this achievement, not confined to Spain, will reach the continents beyond the seas and gladden the hearts of millions who believe that the New World discovered by Columbus is the home of freemen and not of slaves.

On the morning of the 26th of November General Sickles asked for his passports, preparatory to closing the legation and leaving Spain. In the afternoon of the same day he received a note from Señor Carvajal, conceding in part, and conditionally,—at least on paper,—the demands of the United States that the *Virginius* and the survivors should be given up, the perpetrators of the massacre tried and punished, and the flag of the United States saluted. The subsequent details were arranged in Washington between the Secretary of State and the Spanish minister; and the *Virginius* and the survivors of the crew and passengers were surrendered to the authorities of the United States on the 15th of December. On her way to this country she was lost in a storm off Cape Fear.

This affair has been presented at considerable length because it has thus far been the most critical and exciting international event in the history of Cuba, and because it offers an illustration of so many points in the affairs of the island, especially of the dangers that may arise when the just and humane intentions of a central government are frustrated by remote subordinates and hot-blooded populace.

Considerable sums were paid by Spain as compensation to the families of American citizens and British subjects executed at Santiago; but the governor who ordered the executions was never punished. The amount paid over, in order to be distributed among the families of American sufferers, was $80,000.

The *Virginius*, although the most conspicuous, was not the only victim of the Spanish mismanagement in Cuba. During 1877 the three whaling vessels, *Ellen Rizpah*,

Rising Sun and *Edward Lee* while pursuing their legitimate business under the American flag, outside of Cuban waters, were fired upon and detained for days, with circumstances of peculiar hardship and brutality. The United States Government carefully investigated the cases and asked an aggregate indemnity of $19,500, but, in that indulgent spirit which marks its foreign policy, accepted $10,000.

CHAPTER VII.

DURING the succeeding years of the war, the situation in Cuba, the accumulating claims of American citizens for spoliation suffered there, and the progressive exhaustion of both parties to the strife, engaged the most earnest attention of the Government of the United States, which was, however, disposed to proceed with extreme lenity and caution. The Secretary of State, Hamilton Fish, on the 5th of November, 1875, addressed a dispatch (No. 266) to Caleb Cushing, then Minister to Spain. That document,* after recapitulating a number of private claims, long outstanding, entered into a general statement of the Cuban case and urged the necessity that something be done to restore peace to the distracted island. The course contemplated was the most gentle and soothing possible —merely to persuade the combatants to come

*See Appendix B.

to an understanding and agreement, satisfactory to both, and of universal advantage. This celebrated No. 266 was also to be read in confidence to the proper members of the cabinets of Paris, London, Berlin, St. Petersburg, Vienna, and Rome, with a view to inducing those governments, or some of them, to add their friendly voices in favor of pacification.

The whole Cuban situation was again reviewed,* and mediation proposed, in President Grant's annual message of December 7, 1875, but without any direct or visible effect. Still these repeated efforts on the part of the United States may have had some influence in bringing the Spanish authorities to consent to treat with the revolutionists, as was done at El Zanjón.†

Those who are inclined to be dissatisfied with the present Executive for not declaring at once in favor of the revolutionists of 1895--96 would do well to consider the attitude of the Government in 1875, especially as General Grant was a man whose patriotism and Americanism had been so long and

---

* See Appendix C.   † See Appendix D.

thoroughly tested. The position of an official, high or low, invested with powers for the discharge of specific duties and girt around with laws and obligations, is very different from that of the individual who has no such responsibilities. The private citizen may often feel that something ought to be done when the magistrate cannot see that it is his duty to do it, or to do it in a particular way. On the other hand it is to be remembered that President Grant's amiable intentions and earnest efforts were almost, if not wholly, thrown away, and that the probability of bringing the present contestants to agree upon terms that will be mutually and permanently satisfactory, is very remote.

After the capitulation of El Zanjón in 1878, there were promises and expectations of radical reforms in the administration of Cuba; but the promises were not kept in the sense in which they were accepted, and the expectations were not realized. Perhaps they could not be. The failure will appear more fully when we come to consider the government and finances of the island.* The

* See pp. 183 and 198.

essential features of the case remain the same —the enormous public debt, the consequent heavy and complicated taxation, the high salaries of officials, the corrupt administration, and the entire absence of responsibility to those who pay the money. Señor Pérez Castañeda said in the Spanish Senate, June 24, 1891:

The debt of Cuba was created in 1864 by a simple issue of $3,000,000, and it now amounts to the fabulous sum of $175,000,000. What originated the Cuban debt? The wars of Santo Domingo, of Peru, and of Mexico. But are not these matters for the Peninsula? Certainly they are matters for the whole of Spain. Why must Cuba pay that debt?

El Globo of Madrid, October 27, 1891, said:

The debt has gone on increasing, although from 1878 to the 30th of June, 1891, $115,336,304 has been paid for interest and redemption.

The national debt was at that time stated at $1,211,453,696. The annual payment for interest and sinking fund was:

The Spanish share, ...	$56,752,355
The Cuban share, ...	10,435,183
Total, ...	67,187,538

In addition to the permanent debt were the high salaries and the peculations already alluded to, injudicious expenditures, and estates in mortmain. Señor Romero Robledo, in a debate in the Congreso de Diputados at Madrid, after reading a report of malfeasances in the government of Habana, added:

I do not intend to read the whole of the report; but I must put the House in possession of one fact. To what do these defalcations amount? They amount to the following sum : twenty-two millions, eight hundred and eleven thousand, five hundred and sixteen pesos ($22,811,516). Did not the Government know this? What has been done?—*Diario de las sesiones de Cortes*, May 28, 1890.

A speech of General Pando, delivered in the same legislative body, March 8, 1890, and published in the *Época* of Madrid, foots up a series of these embezzlements and defalcations at $40,000,000,—more than the annual revenue of the island. Señor Castañeda said in the same House, June 24, 1891:

How can anyone doubt that corruption exists in the island of Cuba? General Prendergast has furnished your Excellency, or the Directory of your department, with a list of 350 persons employed in the customhouse and the administration against whom proceedings have been taken for fraud, and not one of them has been punished.

In an article by Deputy Dolz in the *Ateneo de Madrid* in the spring of 1895, it was alleged that the customhouse frauds in Cuba since the peace of 1878 amounted to $100,000,000. Rafael de Eslava of Habana, in his " Juicio Crítico de Cuba en 1887," thus summed up his judgment:

Granted the correctness of the points which I have just presented, it seems to be self-evident that a curse is pressing upon Cuba, condemning her to witness her own disintegration, and converting her into a prey for the operation of those swarms of vampires that are so cruelly devouring us, deaf to the voice of conscience, if they have any; it will not be rash to venture the assertion that *Cuba is undone ; there is no salvation possible.*

There was another cause of unrest and discontent, not chargeable to the Spanish Government, but too important to be passed over. It is the increasing production, and consequent diminishing price of the leading articles upon which Cubans have to depend. The principal of these is sugar, the market for which is now disputed by the same article derived from other sources.

The manufacture of sugar from beets may be said practically to have had its beginning in 1830. Even so late as 1853 the yield from that source was only about 200,000 tons; but it has now for many years attained a national, and even international importance. The introduction of improved methods, after the abolition of slavery in Cuba, greatly increased the output in that island; but, while other countries gave encouragement to home production by bounties, drawbacks, or import duties, the Cuban planter had to contend with a heavy tax on his crop, a heavy duty on the machinery for preparing it, a light export duty, and a duty at the port of destination. The following table shows the world's production of beet sugar for the past five years, and the percentage thereof furnished by the German Empire:

1891,	.	.	. 3,501,920
1892,	.	.	. 3,442,198
1893,	.	.	. 3,889,535	39 per cent.
1894,	.	.	. 4,792,530
1895,	.	.	. 4,270,000

The *Review of the Sugar Trade* in 1894 estimated the world's annual production of sugar at 8,100,000 tons—a production that had so far outrun the demand as to leave a surplus of 1,000,000 tons on the market. In the 40 years from 1853 to 1893 the production of cane sugar had increased $2\frac{1}{2}$ fold, that of beet sugar 20 fold. The following table shows the production of cane sugar for a series of years, and the percentage thereof furnished by Cuba:

YEARS.	TONS.	PER CENT.
1880	1,979,900	25.
1881	2,044,000	24.47
1882	2,056,000	23.6
1883	2,210,400	25.4
1884	2,260,100	27.7
1885	2,232,000	27.64
1886	2,503,000	25.
1887	2,501,735	27.6
1888	2,818,708	21.
1889	2,069,464	21.1
1890	2,554,536	27.75
1891	3,124,525	28.
1892	3,045,486	27.3
1893	3,490,469	31.
1894	3,529,849	29.6
1895	2,847,700	10.5

During the same period, the annual wholesale prices of sugar in the New York market have been as follows:

YEARS.	Raw Centrifugals, cents per Pound.	Soft Standard A, cents per Pound.	Hard Granulated, cents per Pound.
1878	7.25	8.94	9.30
1879	6.93	8.53	8.81
1880	7.88	9.48	9.80
1881	7.62	9.84	9.70
1882	7.29	8.87	9.35
1883	6.79	8.14	8.65
1884	5.29	6.37	6.75
1885	5.19	6.06	6.53
1886	5.52	5.81	6.23
1887	5.38	5.66	6.02
1888	5.93	6.69	7.18
1889	6.57	7.59	7.89
1890	5.57	6.00	6.27
1891	3.92	4.47	4.65
1892	3.32	4.21	4.35
1893	3.69	4.72	4.84
1894	3.24	4.00	4.12

Under the present trend of events, taxation remaining the same, it would not be long before Cuban sugar would be excluded from the markets of the world.

In the struggle for the survival of the fittest—that is, the fittest to survive under the circumstances—Cuban tobacco has fared little better than Cuban sugar. In a report of the British consul at Habana in the spring of 1895, the decline in the tobacco trade is shown for six years. The export of cigars, rated at $40 per 1000, amounted

In 1889, to	.	.	.	.	$10,019,040
In 1890, to	.	.	.	.	8,472,920
In 1891, to	.	.	.	.	7,866,560
In 1892, to	.	.	.	.	6,668,480
In 1893, to	.	.	.	.	5,894,600
In 1894, to	.	.	.	.	5,368,400

The decline is due to general taxation, the export duty of $1.80 per 1000, and increasing competition in other countries, especially the United States.

CHAPTER VIII.

THE causes indicated in the foregoing pages have within these 30 or 40 years led to the voluntary, or involuntary, exile of a large number of Cubans, although the natural resources of the island have been more than sufficient for all her children. There are said to be 40,000 in the United States, there are active juntas in the British Islands, and they are also dispersed through the West Indies and Latin America.

While peaceable residents, they are not unmindful of their former home; and have at heart what they suppose to be for its best interests. The Spanish Government naturally complains that the peace of the island is constantly disturbed or threatened by persons outside of its borders; but the causes which placed them outside should be taken into account. The complaint, too, lies against every free country that is geographically accessible; and the right of asylum for political offenders has been exercised for more than 3000 years. No doubt active men in the several foreign countries sometimes communicate and concert with each other and with their friends at home; but for that there is neither remedy or responsibility until some overt act is committed.

In such a manner a rising in Cuba was concerted about the close of 1894. The chief organizer was José Martí, then in New York. The time set for a public demonstration was February 24, 1895. Martí chartered three vessels, the *Lagonda*, the *Amadís*, and the *Baracoa*, and sailed with men and war materials. The expedition was stopped at Fernandina, Fla., by the United States authorities. About the end of January, Martí left New York for Santo Domingo, there to join Máximo Gómez, who had been a military leader in the former war. These and other Cuban leaders seem not to have reached the island before the month of May, and, when the appointed day— February 24—arrived, only 24 men defied the authorities at Ybarra in the province of Matanzas. Martial law had been proclaimed throughout the island the day before. The small number of the insurgents and the absence of recognized leaders seem at first to have deceived the Spanish authorities into a belief that the whole was little more serious than a negro riot, and would be speedily suppressed, as Spain had then in the island an army of 19,000 men, in addition to so many of the 59,000 volunteers as it might be necessary to call out.* Still, to make quite sure, an additional force of 7000 was sent over in the early days of March.

The months of March and April were eventful. Before the arrival of any of the principal leaders, the rebels were rather gaining ground. Events did not move pleas-

---

* The following is from pp. 754–55 of the Spanish Army List (*Anuario Militar de España*) for 1896, and may be taken as an official statement of the strength of the armed forces on duty in Cuba at the outbreak of the insurrection :

"The strength of the permanent army of the Island of Cuba is fixed for the fiscal year 1894–95 at 13,842 men, to which are to be added 4560 of the Civil Guard, 976 of the *Orden Público*, and 943 of the Corps of Volunteers paid from the war section of the Budget for the island.

"The Civil Guard is organized into a General Sub-Inspectorate comprising 3 regiments, each composed of 4 battalions. The total strength is 26 companies and 13 squadrons, with 25 field officers, 166 company officers, 3270 infantry *Guardias*,

antly for the Government at Madrid. Its representative at Washington was recalled, and another sent in his place. Captain General Emilio Calleja Isasi had to be recalled, and was succeeded by General Arsenio Martínez de Campos y Antón, who had ended the previous insurrection by negotiation rather than by force of arms. He arrived in Cuba with fresh re-enforcements about the 10th of April. Later in the month the brothers Antonio and José Maceo, together with Crombet, Cebreco, and some 20 more revolutionary leaders arrived from Costa Rica. Ten days later José Martí, the acknowledged head and general-in-chief of

and 1130 cavalry *Guardias* with 1125 horses. At their head is a brigadier general with the title of sub-inspector general.

" The Corps of *Orden Público* has 2 field officers, 21 company officers, and 919 infantrymen, with 2 company officers and 57 guards in the mounted section.

"In addition to the above forces, there is the *Habana* Battalion of White Militia, the *España* Battalion of Colored Militia, the mounted militia of Habana and of Matanzas, and finally the Corps of Volunteers, which numbers 37 battalions of Infantry, 2 battalions and 1 mounted brigade of Artillery, 12 regiments of Cavalry, and 2 companies of Guides, with a total of 59,114 men, permanently armed, and maintained at their own expense (excepting trumpeters and quartermaster sergeants, who are paid out of the Budget of the island)."

the insurrection, Máximo Gómez y Báez, the present general-in-chief, Borrero, and Angel Guerra arrived from Santo Domingo. The movement, whether revolt or revolution, was thus fairly launched, and has now (May 1, 1896) been going on fourteen months.

Early in the course of the disturbance an incident occurred which caused a sudden flurry in the public mind in the United States, very excusable in those who remembered the events of the last "unpleasantness" in Cuba. The events, perhaps, cannot be told better than in the words of President Cleveland in his annual message of December 2, 1895:

One notable instance of interference by Spain with passing American ships has occurred. On March 8 last, the *Alliança*, while bound from Colón to New York, and following the customary track for vessels near the Cuban shore, but outside the three-mile limit, was fired upon by a Spanish gunboat. Protest was promptly made by the United States against this act as not being justified by a state of war, nor permissible in respect of a vessel on the usual paths of commerce, nor tolerable in view of the wanton peril occasioned to innocent life and property. The act was disavowed, with full expression of regret, and assurance of non-recurrence of such just cause of complaint, while the offending officer was relieved of his command.

That is about the whole of the *Alliança* affair; and if we contrast it with that of the *Virginius*, and suppose the two to be at all characteristic of their respective dates, they afford a most encouraging example of human progress.

Active military operations have to be discontinued during the rainy season, from the end of April to the end of October, on account of the state of the roads and the prevalence of fevers engendered by the heat and dampness. The muddy trails of the country become impassable for large bodies of men and material, while small parties of insurrectionists steal through the mountain paths with which they are familiar. Under such circumstances, which have been more or less present from the beginning, it would be useless to try to detail battles that were only skirmishes, and of which accounts are meager and open to suspicion of partiality. Martí was killed in action May 19, and Gómez assumed the chief command. The Spanish forces are always at least twice as strong numerically as their opponents; and the disparity in point of equipment is still greater. While the interest, therefore, of the one party is to come to a pitched battle,—a fair stand-up fight, once for all,—it is the equally legitimate policy of the other to avoid such trial of strength. A Macedonian phalanx might trample down everything that would be accommodating enough to get in its way and stay there; but a good corps of sharp-shooters would pick off every man of them without receiving a scratch. So it has been a constant reproach by the Spaniards that the rebels would not stay still long enough to be killed.

The first concentration of the rebellion was in the province of Santiago de Cuba, the most mountainous and intricate and the most remote from the capital. Thence the insurrection spread westward. In November the revolutionists were operating in the province of Puerto Príncipe. For reasons to be shown presently, Gómez issued orders that the sugar crops should be everywhere destroyed; and thereupon it became the first duty of General Martínez de Campos to prevent the destruction.

There is a line of forts known as the *trocha* (*i. e.*, trench or traverse) across the island between the provinces of Puerto Príncipe and Santa Clara. Garrisons were placed in these, and the intervals were occupied by small detachments of troops. General Martínez de Campos had conceived the plan of this line of defense in a moment of inspiration during the previous ten years' war, which he had terminated successfully; and now, occupying it again with 100,000 men at his command, he felt confident of being able to say, " Hitherto shalt thou come, but no further." Yet the insurgents under Gómez and Maceo were able to slip through, and return with captured arms and supplies, spreading havoc far and wide, and alarm still more widely. The idea of a *trocha* to fence out an enemy was still thought to be good in itself, but this one was adjudged to be too remote; so a second was drawn through Las Cruces and Las Lajas, skirting the great salt marsh of Zapata. When that proved equally ineffectual, General Martínez de Campos retreated in the direction of the capital, and constructed a third and shorter military line directly across the island from Matanzas to the bay of La Broa. As a further precaution, he placed on the railroad from Habana to Batabanó hundreds of freight cars, which were plated with boiler iron, with loop-holes pierced for rifles. These were filled with soldiers, and kept running at intervals day and night. But these obstacles were overcome like the others, a portion of the railroad track was torn up, and General Maceo, with his division of the insurgent army, moved westward into the rich tobacco region of Pinar del Río, where preparations had been made for his friendly reception.

General Martínez de Campos, with a large, disciplined, and well-appointed army, had thus repeatedly committed the grave military offense of being outgeneraled by what some would fain have us believe to be only a handful of negroes, too illiterate to read the names on the street signs. Such partisans seem not to reflect that the more they belittle the insurgents the more they dishonor the Spanish troops that can make no head against them.

The Spanish forces kept falling back upon Habana, which created so great dissatisfaction at Madrid and among the " peninsulars " that Martínez de Campos was recalled. He sailed for Spain on the 17th of January, his place being temporarily filled by General

Sabas Marín; and on the 10th of February he was succeeded by General Valeriano Weyler y Nicolau, Marquis of Tenerife, whose character the Cuban sympathizers have sought to blacken with the odious and antiquated vice of relentless cruelty. No doubt more energy and success were expected of him than were found in his predecessor; but it is not likely that he is quite so nearly a cannibal as he is represented. He has now (June, 1896) been four months on the island, clothed with *legal* omnipotence, and we have heard of no remarkable success yet, nor is it likely that there will be before November.

During all this time there are reported assurances that, as soon as further re-enforcements arrive from Spain, Captain General Weyler will take the field in person, and show how easily local disturbances can be quelled by one who knows how. In the meantime he too has tried his hand at fence-building. He has established a fourth *trocha* across the island from Majana to Mariel, about 25 miles west of Habana. As this particular barrier is the one most in interest at present, it may be described more particularly. It consists of a ditch, as the name *trocha* would indicate,

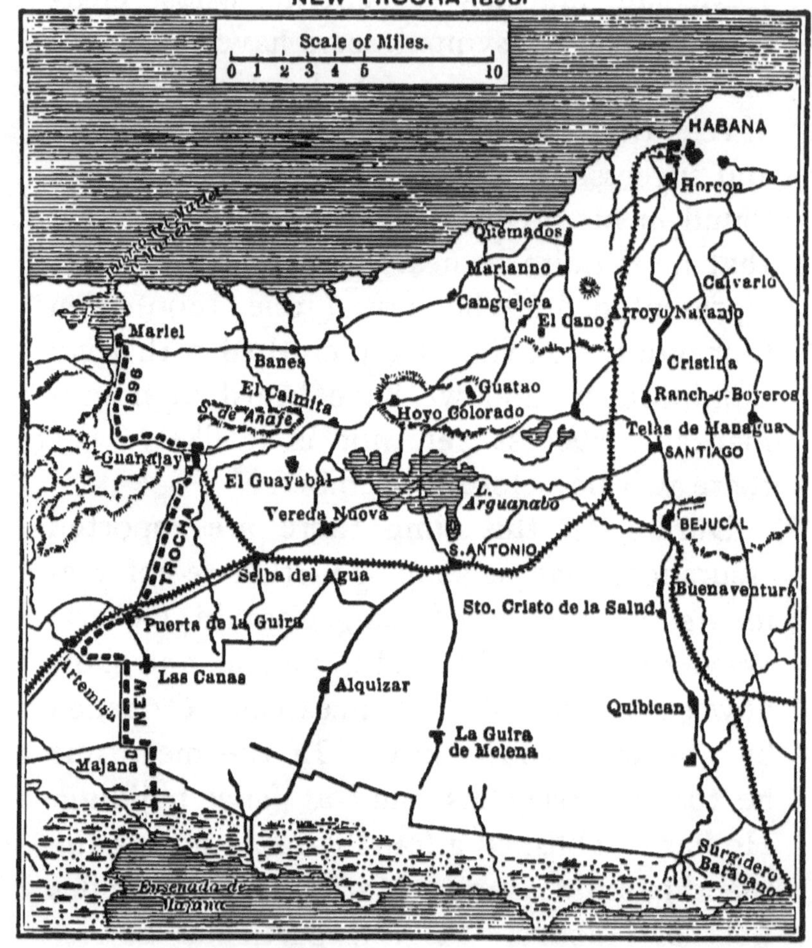
NEW TROCHA 1896.
Scale of Miles.
0 1 2 3 4 5 10
HABANA
Horcon
Quemados
Marianno
Cangrejera
Calvario
El Cano
Arroyo Naranjo
Mariel
Banes
Guatao
Cristina
El Caimita
Ranch-o-Boyeros
S. de Añafe
Hoyo Colorado
Telas de Managua
SANTIAGO
Guanajay
El Guayabal
L. Arguanabo
Vereda Nueva
BEJUCAL
TROCHA
S. ANTONIO
Selba del Agua
Buenaventura
Puerta de la Guira
Sto. Cristo de la Salud
Artemisa
NEW
Las Canas
Alquizar
Quibican
Majana
La Guira
de Melena
Surgidero
Batabano
Ensenada de
Majana

nine feet deep, containing water in the low places. On each bank is a wire fence, and on the east side is a beaten road, which is patrolled by cavalry and light artillery. Along the west bank are detached earthworks, guarded by troops and connected by telephone. The approaches to both sides are protected by rifle pits, about 70 feet apart, and screened by a line of *trous-de-loup*. Interviewers report that the governor congratulates himself very much on his success in fencing the rebels in. On two points, however, better information is needed: whether Maceo has any wish to leave Pinar del Río; and whether he would have any difficulty in doing so, if he tried.

General Weyler has at his disposal at least 120,000 regulars, 50,000 volunteers as home guard, and a large naval coast guard. The figures puzzle the lexicography of the world, to determine whether that is *war* or the *chase of the legal authorities after a bandit horde.*

According to official figures obtained from Madrid, there were in Cuba at the beginning of the insurrection, in February, 1895:

<table>
<tr><td>

15 battalions (60 companies) of Infantry,
2 regiments (8 squadrons) of Cavalry,
1 battalion (4 companies) of Fortress
    Artillery,
1 battery of Mountain Artillery,
1 battalion (4 companies) of Engineers,
3 regiments of *Guardia Civil,*
1 battalion of *Orden Público,*
1 Disciplinary Brigade,
1 Sanitary Brigade,
Various bodies of local troops and special
    corps,

</td><td>19,378</td></tr>
</table>

From the beginning of the outbreak, until
March 10, 1896 (the date of the latest official
returns available), nine successive bodies of
re-enforcements had been sent over, aggregating 121,326 men, in the following proportions of grade:

General officers, ...	40
Field officers, ...	562
Company officers, ...	4,768
Sergeants, ...	3,396
Corporals and privates, . . .	112,560
Total, ...	121,326

thus making the largest military force ever
transported by sea. The strength of the
several expeditions, and the dates at which
they were embarked, are as follows:

1st Expedition (March 8 to March 21, 1895),	.	8,593
2d " (April 1 to April 19, 1895), .	.	7,477
3d " (April 24 to May 8, 1895), .	.	4,008
4th " (May 20 to June 10, 1895), .	.	2,962
5th " (June 18 to July 21, 1895), .	.	9,601
6th " (July 31 to September 30, 1895), .		29,055
7th " (October 5 to November 30, 1895),		26,639
8th* " (December 10, 1895, to January 28, 1896), ...		9,033
9th* Expedition (February 12 to March 10, 1896),		22,432
2 battalions Chasseurs from Puerto Rico, .	.	1,526

Total, ...	.	121,326

Adding this total to that of the original permanent force, we obtain 140,704 as the strength† of the Spanish troops over which General Weyler took command upon his arrival—losses deducted.

The losses in the present Cuban campaign, up to January 16, 1896, according to the records of the Spanish Medical Corps, are as follows:

---

* In making up the quotas for the latest re-enforcements, deserters, fugitives from the draft (*prófugos*), and men under light sentences were pardoned and enrolled.

† To this number must be added such of the Cuban Volunteers as had been mobilized—given in official reports as 5500.

Killed in action,	.	.	.	.	.	286
Died from wounds,	.	.	.	.	.	119
" " yellow fever (*vómito*)			.	.	.	3,190
" " other diseases,			.	.	.	282
Total,	.	.	.	.	.	3,877

The total number admitted to hospital during this period was 7708.   The losses, therefore, if these statements are accurate, have been relatively slight, compared with those of the campaign of 1869--78.*

It may aid us in appreciating the magnitude of Spain's military operations, if we glance at the armament sent over since the outbreak of the insurrection.   Omitting field pieces and heavy ordnance, there have been sent, according to official returns:

INFANTRY AND CAVALRY SMALL ARMS.

64,125 Spanish Mauser magazine rifles, caliber 7 mm., model 1893.

1,176 Spanish Mauser magazine rifles, caliber 7.65 mm.

69,639 Remington repeating rifles, caliber .43 in., model 1871–89.

10,000 Remington repeating rifles, caliber .43 in., model 1871.

5,027 Mauser carbines, caliber 7 mm., model 1893.

* See p. 126.

AMMUNITION.

33,660,000 cartridges for Mauser 7 mm. rifle and carbine.
 7,441,273   "   "   "   7.65 mm. rifle.
13,725,520   "   . "   Remington rifle, model 1871–89.
 7,051,575   "   "   "   "   "   1871.

NOTE.—These figures include what was carried by the troops.

CHAPTER IX.

THE numbers of the revolutionists cannot
be ascertained with any certainty. They
have been variously stated to be from 30,000
to 50,000 men,* but the former is no doubt

*The Habana correspondent of *Le Temps* (Paris) furnished
that paper with the following statement of the strength and
distribution of the insurgent forces at the end of December, 1895:

Máximo Gómez, in Matanzas, ...	5,000 men
Antonio Maceo, in Matanzas, ...	4,000 "
José Maceo, in Santiago de Cuba, . . .	3,000 "
Lacret, in Santa Clara, ...	2,500 "
Núñez, in Habana, ...	1,600 "
Roloff, in Santa Clara, ...	1,500 "
Rego, in Matanzas, ...	1,500 "
Rabí, in Santiago de Cuba, ...	1,000 "
Cortina, in Santa Clara, ...	1,000 "
Quintín Banderas, in Sancti-Spíritus, . . .	1,000 "
Bermúdez, in Habana, ...	500 "
Pancho Pérez, in Santa Clara, ...	800 "
Perico Díaz, in Santa Clara, ...	500 "
Basilio Guerra, in Las Villas, ...	800 "
Lino Pérez, in Trinidad, ...	700 "
Castillo, in Sagua, ...	500 "

nearest the truth. As their object is not fighting, they do not need large armies. Stigmatizing them as " negroes " is, in part at least, an appeal to the prejudice not yet extinct in this country; but Captain Wm. F. Mannix of Washington City, who has just returned from Cuba, and who had the rare opportunity of mixing among them, stated

Vidal, in Sagua, ...	600 men
Cebreco, in Santiago de Cuba, ...	500 "
Zayas, in Habana, ...	500 "
Rafael Socorro, in Cienfuegos, ...	200 "
Ruen, in Guantánamo, ...	200 "
Miró, in Santiago de Cuba, ...	400 "
Ignacio Suárez, in Sagua, ...	200 "
Juan Bravo, in Trinidad, ...	200 "
Pajarito, in Remedios, ...	200 "
Muñoz, in Cienfuegos, ...	50 "
Clotilde García, in Cárdenas, ...	600 "
Luis Chapotín, in Cárdenas, ...	400 "
Perico Cardenos, in Cárdenas, ...	500 "
Robau, in Cárdenas, ...	500 "
R. Carrillo, in Matanzas, ...	400 "

30,750 men

A dispatch to the United Press, dated Habana, March 14, 1896, gave a somewhat similar distribution list, with a total of 42,800 men. This dispatch was read in full in the United States Senate, and published in the Congressional Record for March 23, 1896, on p. 3424.

their proportions at 40 per cent. white, 40 per cent. negro, and 20 per cent. of mixed blood—*i. e.*, just half and half.

The leaders who have thus far shown the highest capacity are Máximo Gómez and Antonio Maceo. The former, now 73 years of age, is a native of Santo Domingo, but took an active part in the revolutionary attempt of 1868. The Maceo brothers are half-breeds, both parents being mulattoes. They have been represented as negroes, wholly uneducated; but Captain Mannix, who exhibits with some pride a *machete* received from the hand of Antonio, describes him as of superb physical development, a gentleman of attractive manners, and not only a dashing cavalry commander but a man of unusual attainments, and even habits of study. It is hoped that General Sheridan will not be disturbed in his cerements by the suggestion of a slight resemblance. If it be said that the rebels are poor, obscure, and not the " solid men " of the island, that charge is so true of all revolutionary movements, and so trite, that we may wonder at the feeble intelligence of anyone who would repeat it. Bankers, brokers, importers, and government contract-ors are not the men to sleep in the woods or trudge at the tail of revolutionary cannon.

In conducting the present war the object of Spain is naturally to suppress the revolt by any means available, and as speedily as pos-sible. The rebels do not wish to shed blood; and they are not straitened for time. They strike at the enemy's weakest point. They war not against flesh and blood, but against Spain's financial credit. Every fall in the market value of Spanish securities, every def-icit in the revenue, every month's pay of the army in arrear, every unpaid bill for transpor-tation and supplies, is to them an indirect victory more acceptable than a dozen inno-cent Spanish youths left dead on the field. Hence the burning of sugar cane is not a mere insane act of barbarism, but one of deliberate policy. The planter whose crop is destroyed cannot pay his income tax; and as he has nothing to send abroad, he can buy no foreign goods to pay duty at the custom-house. This is given as an explanation, not as a justification. The acts of domestic war-fare can seldom be justified. Minister

Dupuy de Lome, in his article in the New York *Herald* of February 23, 1896, seems either not to understand the subject fully or not to state it fully, as he limits the loss on the part of Spain to the small export duty. Yet he is so far aware of its importance as to say in speaking of General Martínez de Campos: " He knew perfectly well that if the sugar crop could be gathered, the backbone of the insurrection would be broken." That being the real point in dispute, success has thus far inclined to the side of the insurgents; for, while Cuba produced in 1894 1,040,000 tons of sugar, the crop of 1895 was only 300,000 tons. (See table on p. 147.)

When prisoners are taken by the Spaniards they are sent to the Isle of Pines for confinement, or to the penal colony of Ceuta on the coast of Africa. Those taken by the Cubans are disarmed and allowed to go. The rifle and cartridge-box are more important than the man who bears them. There have been some exchanges of prisoners, but they have been few. With the imperfect information obtainable, it would be rash to say that none are ever shot on either side.

Notwithstanding the vigilance of the coast guard, military supplies have sometimes reached the island, and some are captured from the enemy. The proportion of each is unknown. When the insurgents have been denied the freedom of a town, and capture it, they help themselves to what they want and can find; but among their friends in the country districts they are furnished gratuitously with food, clothing, and horses.

When it is said that the revolutionists occupy certain provinces, it is not to be understood that they carry on or control all the functions of local government, but only that they move unhindered, and do whatever they undertake, except in the large towns.

Martí, the organizer of the revolution, upon landing in Cuba, issued a call for a constitutional convention. It was on the 13th of September, and long after Martí's death, that the convention met at Camagüey. There were present representatives from all the provinces except Pinar del Río, 20 in all, and 20 from the several divisions of the army. On the 16th of September a constitution was completed and adopted. Two

days later the convention elected the following officers of state:

President.—Salvador Cisneros Betancourt, who had
held the same position in the former revolutionary
government.

Vice President.—Bartolomé Masó, a prominent citizen
of Manzanillo.

Secretary of State for Foreign Affairs.—Rafael Por-
tuondo y Tamayo, a member of a wealthy and distinguished family of Santiago de Cuba.

Secretary of War.—Carlos Roloff of Santa Clara, a
native of Poland, who had come to Cuba in his youth,
and had borne a part in the previous struggle.

Secretary of the Treasury.—Severo Pina, of an old
and wealthy family of Sancti Spiritûs.

General-in-Chief—Máximo Gómez y Báez, the brain
and will of the insurrection.

Lieutenant General.—Antonio Maceo.

The convention also passed laws dividing
the island into States, districts, and pre-
fectures, regulating marriages, establishing
post offices, and providing for the collection
of taxes. In some places local officers have
been installed. The whole is tolerably complete on paper; and yet it would seem that the
powers and functions of the new government
must still be to a great extent in abeyance.
We have no definite and reliable information

whether the President and heads of departments have offices, clerks, and records, or to what extent they discharge the functions usually associated with their titles.

The headquarters of the insurgents is called Cubitas, and is the top of a mountain 25 miles from Puerto Príncipe. It is extremely difficult of access in the face of even very slight opposition. For a considerable distance the pathway is a mere spiral fillet wound round the side of a steep mountain, too narrow in places for horsemen to ride abreast, and a dozen men could defend it against the armies of Xerxes. The top of the mountain is tolerably level, and embraces more than a square mile of arable land, where corn, sweet potatoes, and the other island products are raised. Here the revolutionists have a center of communication, temporary wooden buildings, and a dynamite factory. If held by a small body of resolute men, the place would be equally difficult to storm or starve. It is curious to observe that these West Indian wars are all on the same pattern, determined by climate and topography. That was especially true of the most instructive of them all, the Maroon war in Jamaica, which will be referred to again at greater length. The Maroons, as will be seen, held a similarly inaccessible mountain fastness, from which they defied the English Government for 74 years.

PART III

POLITICAL AND COMMERCIAL.

By M. M. Ramsey, A. M.

POPULATION.

WHILE the area of Cuba and its dependent islands is nearly as great as that of Pennsylvania,* it has less than one-third as many inhabitants as the " Keystone State." Yet when we bear in mind that the desert sandkeys that skirt the island, the impassable swamps that line its south coast, and the rugged and unexplored uplands of its eastern extremity, altogether occupy fully one-fifth of its area, we may conclude that Cuba is fairly well inhabited. Estimating its habitable area at 32,500 square miles, we see that

* Area of Pennsylvania, 45,215 sq. m.; estimated population in 1894, 5,550,550. Area of Cuba, 43,124 sq. m.; estimated population in 1894, 1,723,000.

it is twice as densely populated as the State of Missouri,* or in about the same ratio as Virginia.†

Of the aboriginal inhabitants of Cuba, none survived to see the seventeenth century. The present population may be divided into five classes:

1. Natives of Spain—" peninsulars."
2. Cubans of Spanish descent—" insulars."
3. Other white persons.
4. Persons wholly, or in part, of the African race.
5. Eastern Asiatics.

We will begin by reckoning the first three classes together and excluding the fifth entirely—thus obtaining the usual division of whites and negroes. It has been customary to reckon among negroes persons having one-fourth, one-half, or three-fourths white blood; and on the principle of the civil law, *stirps sequitur matrem*, there is no end to the subdivision. This is philosophically unjust, and makes the negro element appear

---

* State of Missouri : area 69,415 sq. m.; population 1,875,-900.

† State of Virginia : area, 42,450 sq. m.; population, 1,705,-198.

larger than it really is. It is also to be
remembered that the blood of the Latin
nations mingles with that of other races
more readily than does the Saxon. We will
now give some statistics of the two main
races at different dates, showing the percentage of negroes:

YEAR.	WHITE.	NEGRO.	PER CENT.
1804	234,000	198,000	45.8
1819	239,830	213,203	47.
1830	332,352	423,343	56.
1841	418,291	589,333	58.4
1850	479,490	494,252	50.75
1860	632,797	566,632	47.
1869	797,596	602,215	43.
1877	985,325	492,249	33.
1887	1,102,689	485,187	30.55

It is especially worthy of note that for
30 or 40 years the negro element has been
both relatively and absolutely decreasing,
and probably at the present time it com-
poses little more than one-fourth of the whole
population. The ratio of the races in the
city of Washington, by the census of 1890,
was 67 per cent. to 33 per cent., so that
negroes are relatively more numerous in the

capital of our own nation than they are in Cuba.

The first negroes introduced into Cuba were, of course, slaves. African slavery had been known in the Spanish peninsula a considerable time before the discovery of America; and when Ovando was sent out as governor of Hispaniola in 1502, he was permitted to carry to the colony negro slaves, born in Seville and other parts of Spain, who had been instructed in the Christian religion.* The recognized laws of Spain in regard to these people were not very severe. The slave was permitted to have his cabin and patch of ground, and certain hours were allowed him for its cultivation. There was always a prospect—possibly remote—of purchasing his freedom. The negroes were of both sexes, and the domestic relation was possible, and pretty generally respected. Besides, religion had a deep hold on the Spanish character; and the Gospel recognized no distinction on account of color. Still law, or profession, is one thing and fact another. Much depended upon the character of the slave-owner; and often quite as

* *Encyclopædia Britannica*, vol. xii. p. 1376.

much on his necessities as on his character. In any case a class of free negroes grew up, the relative numbers of which, at successive dates until the final abolition of slavery, are here shown:

Year.	Slaves.	Free Negroes.
1811	212,000	114,000
1817	225,268	115,691
1827	286,942	106,494
1841	436,495	152,838
1846	323,759	149,226
1849	323,897	164,410
1860	367,370	207,735
1867	344,615	248,703
1869	363,288	238,927
1877	199,094	272,478
1879	171,087	287,827
1887	[none]	485,187

An act of gradual emancipation passed the Spanish Cortes in 1870; but slavery was finally and absolutely abolished in 1886.

Of the white inhabitants of Cuba perhaps about one-fifth are natives of Spain; but that is merely an estimate. These " peninsulars " hold or control all offices of any value, civil, military, or ecclesiastical,* and so have all the

* The Spanish Government has gone to considerable trouble to combat this idea ; and a semi-official publication (*España y Cuba*, Madrid, 1896—see Bibliography, Appendix G) contains

existing opportunities for earning legalized salaries or for obtaining money otherwise. As their voices can alone be heard, Cuba is authoritatively unanimous in favor of the continuance of the present rule.

The number of white persons of other blood than Spanish is trifling, and has been estimated at 10,500.

There is yet another class of the population—the coolies or Asiatic laborers imported from the Philippines. They began to attract the attention of the world when the philanthropists of England were pressing for the abolition of the slave trade. Two ships from Amoy brought to Habana, in 1847, 679 coolies, and from time to time more followed. The statements of their numbers are so conflicting as to be a mere guess; but that guess would put them at 30,000 to 40,000. If a

a list several pages in length of Cubans who hold or have held public office. A gentleman who is a specialist in Cuban genealogies, and is himself connected with a dozen or more of the leading families, has assured the author that the majority of these names are unknown to him, while a large percentage of the remainder represent the Cuban-born sons of " peninsulars" temporarily resident in Cuba. Students of English history will recall the device by which Edward II. came to be born a Welshman.

rose does not lose its fragrance with its name, neither does slavery, by change of designation, become more merciful, but rather less so. Slavery is of many degrees. As it existed in Cuba and in the United States prior to 1861, the slave was assimilated to his master in language, religion, and local customs and traditions. He had the family relation, even if imperfectly maintained, and in a majority of cases was treated with consideration and humanity; but in coolie labor there are no ameliorating circumstances. Pushed to its extreme, as in the guano pits of Peru, it is the most execrable form of slavery that human avarice has ever devised. In 1844 Great Britain endeavored to enforce a regulation that 12 per cent. of those introduced into her colonies should be women—but, if the decree could have been carried into effect, the resulting polyandry might have been even more brutalizing than the original condition. So the coolie remains for life an outcast and an alien, as if he had landed on the shores of another world, where he could never be naturalized. He is bound to work for a term of years for small pay; and at the expiration of his term, he must either leave the island, which he is seldom able to do, or enter into such new contract as the employer may choose to propose.

In connection with this subject it is important to observe that the leaders in the present revolutionary movement confidently assert that natives, of European descent, are capable of enduring any labor on the island that human beings ought to perform; and that they do now perform the most difficult and important kinds of heavy labor.

The most recent official census is that of December, 1887. The figures in the following table are taken from it, and give the population by provinces, as well as the density of population (number of inhabitants per sq. kilo.) in each:

PROVINCES.	INHABITANTS.	SQUARE KILOMETERS.	DENSITY.
Pinar del Río.......	225,891	14,967	15.09
Habana.............	451,928	8,610	52.49
Matanzas...........	259,578	8,486	30.59
Santa Clara.........	354,122	23,083	15.34
Puerto Príncipe.....	67,789	32,341	2.10
Santiago de Cuba....	272,379	35,119	7.76
Totals	1,631,687	122,606	13.31

GOVERNMENT.

Cuba has enjoyed representation in the Spanish Cortes since the passage of the act of January 9, 1879. The province of Habana sends three senators to Madrid, and each of the other five provinces, two; the archbishopric of Santiago sends one, the University of Habana sends one, and the Society of the Friends of the Country, one. Thirty deputies, allotted according to population, are sent to the House of Deputies. These are elected by popular ballot, in the ratio of one representative for every 50,000 inhabitants.

In view of what has been said already, it will be easily understood that the " peninsulars " and the Cuban Volunteers would have great influence in the elections—an influence always adverse to innovation. These conservatives would be likely always to secure a majority. Indeed it is said that out of 30 deputies elected this spring, 26 are natives of Spain. But were they representatives in fact as well as in law, still, on every question involving a conflict of interests, they would be in a hopeless minority—much worse situated than the Irish members in the British parliament. At the very best they can only serve to make the wants of Cuba known—to exercise the right of petition.

The present division of provinces and the corresponding scale of parliamentary representation are regulated by the decree of June 9, 1878. These and the provincial assemblies are the chief of the great reforms promised and accorded at the close of the ten years' war.

The military government has at its head a captain general (*ipso facto* governor general), and under him is an army usually of about 13,000 troops sent from Spain, but paid out of the Cuban budget. He is assisted by a "second chief of the district" who is also sub-inspector general and governor of Habana. Owing to the present disturbed state of the island this force has been increased more than ten-fold and the normal military subdivisions have been entirely rearranged.

Although the decree of 1825 * was revoked about 1870, the captain general retains substantially all that was thereby granted. He

* See p. 101.

is appointed by the Crown, usually for a term of three to five years; has the military rank of lieutenant general; and his full title is governor and captain general. He is the supreme head of the civil, ecclesiastical, military, and naval organizations in the island, and possesses practically the powers claimed by the Turkish Sultan. He is assisted by a council of administration, composed of 30 members—a much vaunted reform of 1895.* The Crown appoints 15 of the members, and the other 15 are elected by the provinces, according to population; though, as elections are controlled, there are likely to be among these latter always as many as 10 peninsulars, or ultra-loyalists, so as to give the Government a safe majority of 25 to 5. To make that point sure, however, the governor general may at any time suspend members likely to give trouble, to the number of 14; or, if the disagreement is too great, he may, after consulting the peculiar body called the " council of authorities," suspend them all, and go on without them. To reduce this elastic council to a do-nothing and mere air-cushion for deadening blows, the members

* Royal decree of March 15, 1895.

serve without pay, yet are personally and pecuniarily responsible to those who may be injuriously affected by their votes. Thus, on every active movement, they are in danger of vexatious and expensive suits for damages. It is this council that is especially relied on to give satisfaction to all parties. It is its duty to do a great many things, such as to prepare the budget, or estimate of receipts and expenditures to be submitted to the Cortes; and to pass resolutions (quasi acts) on all necessary public matters. It is then the duty of the governor general to give effect to these resolutions—if he likes them. If he does not, he suspends them, and takes his own course. It is his duty, however, to keep the Home Government advised of everything of importance, including differences that may arise between himself and the council of administration.

The council of authorities is made up of the Archbishop of Santiago (when present); the Bishop of Habana; the commanding officers of the army and navy; the chief justice of the Supreme Court of Habana; the attorney general; the head of the department of finances; and the director of the local administration. They do not hold regular sessions, but are called together as occasion may require; their conclusions are submitted in writing, but have no binding effect.

The heads of executive departments are distinct from these councils; but heads of departments may be, and are, members of the council of authorities.

The administration in each province is conducted by a governor, appointed by the Crown, who is an officer of the army of the rank of major general or brigadier general, and is directly responsible to the governor general. There is also in each province an elective assembly of not less than 12 nor more than 20 members, according to population. They are elected for four years, and one-half the number are replaced every second year. The elections are held in the first half of September, and sessions twice a year. On meeting, the first business is to ballot for three candidates, from which list the captain general appoints one as speaker. He may, however, disregard the names presented, and appoint any other member.

Moreover the governor of the province may, at his pleasure, preside and vote; and if at any time, in his judgment, the public interest demands it, he may prorogue the assembly and report his action to the governor general. The latter has further the authority to suspend any of the provincial assemblies and report the fact to the Government at Madrid. The provincial governor nominates five members of the assembly to be appointed by the governor general as a local council or cabinet. As, however, the powers and duties of the provincial governments are only equal to those of county boards in the United States, it is easily seen that the home rule accorded to Cuba has its limits.

City governments are formed on the same general pattern as the provincial. The board of aldermen may consist of any number from 5 to 30 inclusive, according to population. They elect one of their number as mayor; but the governor general may substitute any other member.

The judicial system of Cuba includes two superior courts (*audiencias*), one sitting at Puerto Príncipe, for the two eastern provinces, and the other at Habana, for the four western provinces. Inferior to these is a network of judicial districts and local magistracies.

But the judicial system becomes less important to the general reader when it is remembered that the governor general has authority under a decree of June 9, 1878, to overrule any decision of any court, and even to suspend the execution of any law or order emanating from the Government at Madrid.

RELIGION.

The Roman Catholic is the only religion tolerated. There are no Jewish or Protestant places of worship; and while a person who should comply with all other requirements might be permitted to remain on the island, he would not be allowed to promulgate doctrines at variance with those of the established church.* The island formerly

* " No se permitirán otras ceremonias ni manifestaciones públicas que las de la religión del Estado ó sea la católica, apostólica romana."—*Leyes de Imprenta, Reunión y Asociación Vigentes en las Islas de Cuba y Puerto Rico*, Madrid, 1892, p. 59.

constituted a single diocese, that of Santiago; but in 1788 the western part was formed into the diocese of Habana, and in 1804 the Bishop of Santiago de Cuba was elevated to the dignity of archbishop.   The individual clergy are appointed and assigned by these prelates, the captain general taking no immediate part in the matter.

Catholicism being a state religion, its maintenance is made a charge against the general revenues of the island, and all its items are determined at Madrid.   The amount estimated in the Cuban budget of 1893--94 is $385,588, the distribution of which fills 31 quarto pages of that document.

EDUCATION.

The educational system of Cuba is under the direction of the governor general and the rector of the University of Habana, the latter, as well as the former, being a native of Spain and appointed by the Crown.   In 1721 a papal bull authorized the Order of Preaching Friars to establish, in the city of Habana, a university and confer academic degrees; and, with the concurrence of the King of Spain, seven years later, the Royal and Pontifical University was established in the convent of St. John Lateran. In that early age its purpose and studies were largely determined by the Church and the education required of the clergy; and down to 1841 the rectors, with three exceptions, belonged to the monastic orders. The local habitation was a monastery, or buildings erected for that purpose. The corner stone of the new university buildings was laid January 4, 1884. The pontifical part of the title has dropped out, and the institution is now known as The Royal University of Habana. The latest official report before us is for the year 1889--90. It was then divided into the five departments of Philosophy and Letters, Medicine, Pharmacy, Law, and Science. The faculty was made up of 86 professors, including assistant professors, and the number of students who entered for the year was 1046.

There is also a collegiate institute in each of the six provinces, empowered to confer the degree of bachelor or licentiate.

The numbers of students in these were:

Habana, ...	1,752
Matanzas, ...	268
Puerto Príncipe, ...	144
Santa Clara, ...	345
Pinar del Río, ...	145
Santiago de Cuba, ...	255
Total, ...	2,909

Then too there is the Professional School of the Industrial Arts with 53 students, and the Habana School of Painting and Sculpture with 454. An American would be likely to notice the disparity in numbers between the votaries of the fine and those of the industrial arts.

In the year above referred to, the children who attended the public or municipal schools were:

Habana, ...	14,724
Pinar del Río, ...	3,565
Matanzas, ...	5,327
Puerto Príncipe, ...	1,542
Santa Clara, ...	6,917
Santiago de Cuba, ...	6,031
Total, ...	38,106

The children attending the common schools would thus be at the rate of 1 to 45 of the population; or, if the students in the higher institutions be included, the persons receiving instruction outside of institutions of private benevolence, of which there are a considerable number, would be 1 to 40.

The amount estimated for educational purposes was (Budget for 1893--94) $137,-760, no part of which was in aid of any grade of common schools.

The approximate ratio of school and college attendance, of all grades and kinds, for the year 1891--92 is here shown for several countries, that for Spain, however, being no later than 1885:

United States :
North Atlantic Division,	1 to 4.1
South " "	1 " 8.
North Central "	1 " 4.3
South " "	1 " 4.8
Western "	1 " 4.38
Canada,	1 " 5.
United Kingdom,	1 " 5.37
France,	1 " 5.5
Italy,	1 " 9.8
Spain,	1 " 9.
Jamaica,	1 " 7.7
Cuba,	1 " 40.

Education was made compulsory by a law of 1880; but that again is an instance of the difference between law and fact. The law is nugatory where there is not the ability and the disposition to provide schoolhouses and teachers.

CENSORSHIP.*

The publication of anything offensive or disrespectful toward the sovereign or his Government, or having a tendency toward a change of government, is an offense punishable by a fine and imprisonment. There are many varieties and degrees; and much is necessarily left to the discretion and feeling of the courts. To insure immunity, the law imposes upon editors, publishers, etc., very stringent requirements, the neglect or imperfect performance of which is in turn a penal offense.

Every person preparing to start a periodical, must, at least four days before the date of its first number, file with the governor of his province or the mayor of his town, a declaration of his intention. This declaration must show:

* See *Leyes de Imprenta, Reunión y Asociación Vigentes en las Islas de Cuba y Puerto Rico,* Madrid, Centro Editorial de Góngora, 1892.

1. The full title of the periodical and the days of publication.

2. The full names, titles, and places of residence of the manager, the editor, and the printer; and the assurance that neither is under any civil or political disability. The same person may hold two or all of these positions.

3. The name and location of the printing office, and evidence that it is not in arrear for taxes of any kind.

4. When a company is the proprietor, the declaration shall be made by the chief member, who shall furnish evidence that it has been legally organized.

5. In case of changes, all these items of record must be kept up to date, under penalty.

The performance of the foregoing will not exempt other persons who may be implicated [*c. g.,* as authors or contributors] in publishing objectionable articles.

Three copies of every issue must be presented to the governor or mayor, who stamps and returns one, retains one, and sends one to the district attorney to search for seditious matter. In Habana a similar set of three must also be sent to the office of the captain general.

Anonymous publications, however innocent, are not permitted. Everything must show on its face, title, author, and place of publication.

Of pamphlets, as of periodicals, three copies must be submitted to the Government.

Full authority to allow or prohibit pictorial illustrations is vested in the governor general.—Law of November 11, 1886.

A law of June 12, 1888, regulates with much minuteness the formation, management, and governmental control of voluntary associations. Such societies are usually formed for mutual aid and relief, instruction, or entertainment; and the effect of the law can best be shown by following an outline of the steps pursued by an ideal society, *Los Buenos Amigos de Manzanillo*. Its objects are to pay a weekly allowance to its sick members, and hold meetings for business, sociality, music, and poetic recitations. Everything being prepared, the originators submit to the governor of the province documents in duplicate, signed by them and exhibiting the exact title and purposes of the association, copies of its constitution and by-laws, its place of meeting, its sources of income, the character of its expenditures, and the final disposition of its assets in case of dissolution. One copy of these papers is stamped and re-

turned, and the other is kept by the governor
to be examined by his legal adviser. A
meeting, organization, and election of officers are then held and duly reported to the
governor. A notice of each meeting is given
24 hours in advance to the governor, so that
he may be present, if he choose, either in
person or by deputy. He often does either
the one or the other. On one occasion he
breaks up the assembly, and forbids any
further meetings because one of the pieces
sung seems to him to have allusions that
savored of revolution. He is obliged, however, to submit his objection to the superior
court of the district; and twenty days later,
that tribunal decides that there is no
sufficient ground for dissolving the society;
and it goes on. On another occasion the
governor's proxy breaks up a meeting because there are invited guests present, who
are not members. His action is sustained by
the court.

Every time that there is a change of the
place of meeting, of any of the officers or of
any of the by-laws, the ceremony of notifying
the authorities has to be repeated.

Even a private reception of a social nature

cannot lawfully be held without first obtaining a permit.

TRADE AND FINANCE.

Circumstances already presented have led to a system of heavy taxation in Cuba. This is denied by the zealous defenders of Spain; and to verify it would require a thorough exhibition of the revenue systems that apply to Cuba and to half a dozen other countries, which obviously cannot be given here.* A few illustrations, however, may be offered.

Cuba and Jamaica are islands, having nearly the same situation, climate, and productions. Nature has not suggested any difference in their political treatment. The tariff schedules of import duties of the two islands lie before us as we write. That of Jamaica is comprised in 3 printed pages; the Cuban tariff covers 42, which at least suggests a difference in complexity. The larger document contains 417 dutiable articles or classes; the smaller 63 articles, or classes,

* Those who desire precise information on the subject are referred to the *Bulletins Internationaux de Douanes*, issued by F. Hayez, 112 Rue de Louvain, Brussels, Belgium.

dutiable, and 106 free. The rates of duty cannot always be compared, as when articles are reckoned by the yard in one country and by the pound in the other. The following articles are selected from those that admit of comparison, as being fairly representative:

	CUBA.	JAMAICA.
Building stone, per ton	$10.50	$ .00
Marble, per cwt	2.00	.00
Coal, per ton	.75	.00
Salt, per barrel	10.00	2.70
Petroleum, per gallon	.14	.12½
Iron castings, per cwt	1.00	.00
Tiles, per cwt	.81	.00
Butter, per pound	.07½	.00
Cheese, per pound	.11¼	.02
Gunpowder, per pound	.60	.24
Writing paper, per pound	.07	.00
Books, per pound	.07⅘	.00
Agricultural machinery and implements, per cwt	1.13	.00
Horses, common, each	45.00	.00
Cows, each	14.00	.00
Calves, each	10.00	.00
Pianos, each	82.00	.12½ %
Carriages, not specially designated, each	198.00	.12½ %
Steam machinery, per cwt	3.18	.00
Ships, wooden, per registered tonnage, per ton	{ 6.80 / 8.80	.00 / .00

What should equally surprise the general reader is that, of the 417 classes of articles,

254 pay higher duties in Cuba than in the sister isle of Puerto Rico and none pay lower. That has resulted from the bad habit of pledging the revenues of Cuba for the debts incurred by Spain. In comparing these, since the standards of measure and value are the same, the illustration will not be impaired by regarding the kilo as a mere algebraic x:

	CUBA.	PUERTO RICO.
Building stone, per ton................	$10.50	$ 5.00
Coal, per ton......................	.75	.37
Fine earthenware, per 100 kilo.......	9.20	4.60
Steel, fine, in bars, per 100 kilo.....	6.00	3.00
Iron, in bars, per 100 kilo..........	1.25	.75
Tin plate, per 100 kilo..............	5.00	2.50
Articles made of zinc, per 100 kilo...	40.00	20.00
Varnishes, per 100 kilo..............	19.00	9.50
Osnaburgs, ducks, canvas, per 100 kilo.	23.60	12.00
Linen, fine, per kilo................	3.40	1.70
Carpets, cut brussels, per kilo........	.71	.40
Flannel, all wool, per kilo...........	1.32	.70
Hosiery, per kilo....................	3.02	1.55
Furniture, parlor, fine, per kilo......	1.40	.95
Horses, common, each...............	45.00	23.00
Mules, each........................	37.00	22.00
Cows, each	14.00	9.00
Boots, fine, per dozen...............	9.90	5.00
Steam boilers and motors, per 100 kilo.	6.00	3.00
Machinery, per 100 kilo.............	9.50	5.10
Pork, per 100 kilo..................	10.00	5.00

Duties on imports, however, are not the only form in which revenue can be raised; and Spanish necessity has stimulated ingenuity to find things that could be taxed. The following are the estimated sources and amounts of income relied upon by the Cuban budgets (*Presupuestos generales de gastos é ingresos de la Isla de Cuba*) for the fiscal years 1893--94 and 1895--96.

	1893–94.	1895–96.
Tax on real estate	$ 1,711,000	$ 1,711,000
Import duties	9,620,000	9,620,000
Export duties	1,220,000	1,220,000
Port dues	535,000	460,000
Ten per ct. tax on passenger fares.	240,000	240,000
Excise on liquors, sugar,* tobacco, and petroleum	2,580,000	2,130,000
Tax on trades and professions	1,680,000	1,680,000
Stamp tax (including postage and telegraph)	2,174,660	2,174,660
Lotteries	3,104,000	3,104,000
Rents and sales of public property,	399,000	399,000
All other sources	1,377,100	2,017,100
Total	$24,640,760	$24,755,760

The expenditures were estimated as follows:

* Excise on sugar abolished by law of February 20, 1895.

	1893–94.	1895–96.
Interest on the public debt......	$10,435,183	$10,435,183
Salaries and expenses of the Colonial Ministry at Madrid.......	155,125	158,855
Regular army......	4,128,616	4,128,616
Navy........................	1,055,136	1,055,136
Military and naval pensions and retired pay..................	1,746,829	1,746,829
Civil pensions and retired pay...	442,223	442,223
Judiciary.....................	317,595	317,595
Religious establishment.........	385,583	385,583
Volunteers....................	1,768,125	1,768,125
Treasury department...........	708,125	708,125
Police force..................	2,664,923	2,664,923
Executive government, omitting police......................	1,371,165	1,414,665
Department of the Interior......	771,125	778,625
Other expenditures.............	87,636	88,761
Total..................	$26,037,389	$26,093,244

Here note the following points:

1. The *peso*, as compared with the American dollar, is worth only ninety-six cents.

2. The first six items of expenditure, aggregating about $18,000,000, arise from the dependence upon Spain, and are such as British colonies do not have to pay.*

* It is perhaps not generally known to the public that, from the income derived from the Island of Cuba, a fund of $20,000 per annum is set aside "for the secret expenses of the legation at Washington and consulates in the United States," and so

3. The estimates do not include the notorious peculations, an unknown amount, but possibly $10,000,000 more.

4. The levies and appropriations are not made by a Cuban legislature, but everything, down to the salary of the lowest parish priest, is determined at Madrid.

Cuban statistics (always to be taken as approximations) placed the exports between 70 and 71 millions of dollars for the year 1890. The following table (from the *Diario de la Marina*, December 9, 1893) shows the countries to which the exports were sent, and the amount, and the percentage of the whole, taken by each. There is reason to believe that the total exports have been greater since the date indicated, as the average exports to the United States during the five years which ended June 30, 1895, were $66,389,016. During the same period the exports from the United States to Cuba averaged only $17,141,922.

provided in the annual budget. (See *Presupuestos generales de gastos é ingresos de la I. de Cuba* for 1895–96, section 6, chapter xvi., p. 30.)

Cuban Exports in 1890.

	Amount.	Per Cent.
To the United States, . . .	$58,557,641	82.933
" " Spanish Peninsula, . .	8,121,814	11.502
" British America, . . .	995,890	1.410
" France, ...	733,851	1.039
" Germany, ...	657,068	.930
" Great Britain, ...	394,616	.549
" Puerto Rico, ...	269,191	.381
" Colombia, ...	258,008	.365
" Mexico, . . . , .	211,902	.301
" Uruguay, ...	159,522	.226
" the Canary Islands, . .	91,773	.129
" Haití, ...	33,274	.047
" Venezuela, ...	32,768	.047
" Costa Rica, ...	27,497	.039
" All other countries, . . .	64,138	.092
Total, ...	$70,608,953	100.

By far the greatest part of the export trade has been of sugar, which has had to labor under the twofold disadvantage of heavy taxation at home and severe competition from beet sugar abroad.

CUBA AS A NEIGHBOR AND A CUSTOMER.

Countries, like families or towns, may be neighbors, with ample opportunities either to render acts of courtesy and kindness, or to cause annoyance. The latter has been the part of Cuba.

It seems proper here to make a remark or two upon law in general, and the law of nations in particular. Law, however brought about, is a compromise, whereby people delegate, to a power or organization called a government, a part of their rights, the better to preserve the remainder, and have leisure left to attend to their affairs. The government has, or ought to have, power to overcome all resistance to the performance of its delegated trusts. Law is conservative, that is, inclined to regard the thoughts and facts of yesterday rather than those of to-day; and, in treasuring up the wisdom of past ages, it is apt to preserve some of their follies.

International law has the failings of municipal law without its principal advantage. Its terms are vague, involving questions of less or more—of quantity or degree—and the quantity or degree is not measurable. Every nation is the judge of its own honor and safety; that is to say, in most cases the litigants are also the judges. As in the question between Job and the Deity, there is no daysman to lay his hand upon them both.

International law is like a tacit understanding among a company of hunters or gamblers as to what may and what may not be done. If two disagree, their last resort is to fight. The others may counsel peace; they cannot compel it.

If these considerations be just, the force of arguments based upon the law of nations is often more apparent than real. There is no difference in principle between the rights of a man and the rights of a nation. Each has a perfect right to live and improve his or its condition until he or it infringes the equal right of some other. From that point the right begins to diminish until it may cease altogether. " Sacred " and " inalienable " rights belong to the domain of poetry and rhetoric rather than science. There is perhaps no more sacred right than that of a father to the custody and obedience of his child; but if he fail to maintain and teach the child, if he treat it cruelly, overtax its powers, and bring it up to be a menace to the peace of society, his right ceases. It is an old legal maxim that a man's house is his castle, where no one has a right to intrude; but if he be committing a murder, or other felony, therein, the police may break into his castle and stop him.   Nay, may not anyone do so?

Applying these considerations to the case of Cuba, the American people will have to reach the conclusion that Spain's right to the island cannot be greater than her ability and willingness to govern it according to modern civilization.   It is scarcely an extravagance to say that for 40 years Spain has kept a disorderly house at our very door.   It is not sufficient to reply, as a Cuban governor once said in substance, " If you don't like my establishment, keep your young men at home."   That would not avail in a police court.   We object to the temptation.   Nor is it any answer to allege that it is intruders from abroad who are continually disturbing the peace of the island.   All the principal movers are refugees, who have been driven out of Cuba and seek to return.   So far from being a justification, these people are a great part of the wrong.   And be it remembered, there is no similar class of fugitives from the surrounding islands or mainland.

The cases of the *Black Warrior* and *Virginius*, already related, illustrate the annoyance given to American shipping; and numbers of vessels have been fired upon, stopped on the open seas, searched, or seized.* Then there are arrests of American citizens and embargoes on their property. An executive document, before us as we write, contains the names of 66 American citizens executed without due trial during the ten years' war. There are also fines, delays, and restrictions on business that are without excuse. A case is related by Edward Everett, Secretary of State, in a letter to the Comte de Sartiges, December 1, 1852, in which the captain general refused to let the passengers and mail be landed from an American steamer because it had been reported (falsely) that the purser had, in a foreign country, published something that was considered offensive. Rules are made that are minute, burdensome, and vexatious, and arbitrary fines imposed for their infraction. Fines have been imposed for not calling hoops, " wooden hoops," and for not describ-

---

* There were, in particular, the three whaling vessels, *Ellen Rizpah*, *Rising Sun*, and *Edward Lee*, fired upon and stopped in 1877. At this present writing the *Competitor* and all on board are held under circumstances similar to those of the *Virginius*.

ing nails as " iron nails." *   When these vex-
ations are small, they have to be allowed to
pass; when very grave they lead to diplomatic correspondence at a range of 3000
miles, which may last for years before any
redress can be obtained.   It may be concluded then that, under existing circumstances, Cuba is a bad neighbor.

We will next advert to one feature of our
trade with Cuba.   We are far from cherish-
ing any superstitious reverence for either
gold or silver or any other special expression
of value; but thus far money in some form is
an indispensable convenience in carrying on
trade.   As between two countries, if country
A buys largely of country B, and pays cash,
while B will buy nothing from A, there is a
general feeling that the last named is working
under a disadvantage, having to carry its
products somewhere else to obtain money to
pay B.   If, however, A has mines of gold or
silver, those metals are to that extent one of
its normal products.   Otherwise, the general
quest is not to find people willing to sell their
own products, but people who will buy ours.
In most cases there is exchange of commodi-

* *Atlantic Monthly* for July, 1879, p. 84.

ties, with a balance on the one side or the other, and we generally strive to have to pay as small a balance as possible.

Let us see how the case stands between us and the countries most nearly in the same situation with Cuba. The figures are for five years ending June 30, 1895, from the report on " The Foreign Commerce and Navigation of the United States" compiled by the Bureau of Statistics, 1896. We shall, merely for brevity of distinction, call the excess of our imports from any country over our exports " loss," and the opposite balance, " gain ":

British West Indies :

Imports, ...	$67,556,530
Exports, ...	42,230,435
Loss, ...	$25,326,095

French West Indies :

Exports, ...	$9,146,563
Imports, ...	107,606
Gain, ...	$9,038,857

Danish West Indies :

Exports, ...	$2,932,927
Imports, ...	1,949,830
Gain, ...	$983,097

Dutch West Indies:

Exports,	. . . . .	$3,413,262
Imports,	. . . . .	713,252
Gain,	. . . . .	$2,700,010

Haiti:

Exports,	. . . . .	$27,551,472
Imports,	. . . . .	10,768,789
Gain,	. . . . .	$16,782,683

Santo Domingo:

Imports,	. . . . .	$11,015,858
Exports,	. . . . .	6,316,349
Loss,	. . . . .	$4,699,509

Puerto Rico:

Imports,	. . . . .	$15,062,886
Exports,	. . . . .	12,125,896
Loss,	. . . . .	$2,936,990

Cuba:

Imports,	. . . . .	$346,902,092
Exports,	. . . . .	87,269,138
Loss,	. . . . .	$259,632,954

The shipments of gold to Cuba during the same time were $87,544,830; of silver, $298,-256. The remainder must have been settled indirectly, in other ways.

At the same time the trade of Spain with Cuba, regulated by differential duties, showed quite different results. Spanish official statistics for the year ending June 30, 1894, give the following:

Spanish exports to Cuba,	. .	$23,412,376
Spanish imports from Cuba,	.	7,528,622
Difference,	. . . .	$15,883,754

This balance would, for five years, amount to $79,418,770. At least the greater part of this went, or ought to have gone, to remunerate Spanish labor, while the similar toilers of America were out of pocket nearly $260,000,000. It would really seem that, under the existing state of things, Cuba is not much better as a customer than as a neighbor.

Again, Spain does not treat Puerto Rico as she does Cuba:

Spanish exports to Puerto Rico,	.	$5,735,779
Spanish imports from Puerto Rico,		4,316,025
Difference,	. . . .	$1,419,754

CONCLUSION.

The reader who, with exemplary patience, has accompanied us thus far, would no doubt be glad to get some idea as to the final outcome of it all.   But to foresee that outcome would require the gift of prophecy, not granted to mortal men in these ages, and whatever we say can be only an expression of individual opinion.   Several points may be put in the form of questions with partial answers:

1. *Are the revolutionists in Cuba entitled to the rights of belligerents?*

So far as that is a question of international law, its discussion would be too lengthy to be allowed space here.*   So far as it relates to their being a nation, and entitled to recognition as such, in the sense in which Belgium, Denmark, and Portugal are nations, it is evident that they are not, but are more like outlaws in the woods and mountains.   The countries named have completely organized governments, elaborate codes of law and courts for their administration, public rec-

* See Appendix F.

ords, and systems of revenue and expenditure. Their governments exercise control over well-defined territories and all the cities, institutions, persons, and property within their borders. They are obeyed, with scarcely a dissenting voice. They have civil, military, and naval forces, to overcome any possible resistance, and to protect life and property; and they are known and recognized of all men. The revolutionists in Cuba have scarcely a vestige of these attributes.

2. *Will the Cuban revolutionists succeed?*

One who asks such a question usually leaves something unexpressed—that something being: " if all the conditions remain the same." They are not likely to remain the same five or ten years. But if they should, while Spain patrols the coast with a large fleet, and keeps a regular and well-equipped army of 130,000 men in the field and a home guard of 50,000, it does not seem possible for the insurgents to take and hold any considerable city. Still, very similar difficulties were repeatedly overcome by the Spanish-American revolutionists, even when they seemed utterly annihilated, or were driven into unseen hiding places, or even out of their respective countries—as in the case of General O'Higgins after his defeat at Rancagua

3. *Will Spain succeed in suppressing the insurrection?*

Her prospect is not bright. Insurrection is somewhat a matter of climate. Where human life is possible with little food, less clothing, and scarce any shelter; where an enemy can melt into air in one place and materialize the next day in another; when he can disappear into caves or impenetrable jungles, whose paths he alone knows, or ascend mountain heights that can be defended by half a dozen men, such a war may be carried on indefinitely. This is why revolutions are so often attempted in the countries south of us—seldom successful, yet almost impossible to suppress. A few examples are instructive, of which the Maroon war in Jamaica is probably the best. When Jamaica was acquired by the English in 1655, a number of negro slaves of the former French colonists refused to submit to their new masters, and betook themselves to the wilderness. There they maintained a wild, predatory independence 74 years, until hostilities were terminated by a treaty* that distinctly recognized their autonomy.

The Maroons of Guiana and the Araucans of Chile have never been subdued.

4. *Are the disputants likely to come to a peaceful settlement?*

It would seem as if one or the other must be considerably weakened before consenting to a real settlement; so irreconcilable are the rival interests and claims. The revolutionists aim at complete independence; probably not at annexation to the United States. Spain might consent to many changes in the form, but to none in the substance of her governmental machinery. The substance of that rule is absolute control, as much revenue as can be collected, a pasture-ground for needy " peninsulars," and differential duties to favor Spanish industries.

5. *What changes of circumstances may be expected?*

It would be rash to conjecture the moves that may be made on the chess-board of nations within the next five or ten years. One of the least surprising results would be the failure of Spain's resources. It is fine to

* See Appendix E.

talk of spending the last man and the last dollar rather than lose; but it is quite possible to spend the last dollar, without which the last man is of little avail, and still lose. And as to the creditors, it is not to their interest that the struggle should be a protracted one, with Spain getting every year weaker.

6. *Would not a free Cuba become a second Haití with its horrors?*

The African element, supposed to be the one that is feared, is proportionally about one-third as great in Cuba as in the sister isle, and has long been decreasing. If, as it seems, the colored people there be similar to those in the United States, there is nothing to be feared from them. The conduct of the American negroes during the Civil War and since emancipation has been such that the friend of man may point to it with gratification for ages yet to come. If reference be had to the excesses committed in Haití from 1791 to 1820, it is to be remembered that the initiative in falsehood, treachery, and cruelty was given by the Europeans, and that mankind generally are more humane now than they were a century ago. The greatest danger to a free Cuba would be in the rivalries of ambitious leaders.

7. *What is the chief interest of the United States in the matter?*

To have a peaceful, well-behaved neighbor, and a fair, honest customer. Cuba would be a less valuable acquisition now than was once supposed. If it became a State, Territory, or dependency of the Union, the sugar production of Louisiana would be prostrated at a blow, because the season for maturing cane is two months longer on the island than in the State. On the other hand a market would be opened for manufactured goods and the employment of capital, and the greatest provocative to foreign collision would be removed. Again, we ought to hesitate before becoming responsible for the actions of a people whose qualifications for good citizenship have not yet been fairly proved. Neither the Government nor any great number of the thinking people of the United States wish to acquire or disturb Cuba in any way, if it would cease to be a public nuisance. He who will read the Presidential messages, and the diplomatic correspondence of the State Department, will see that our public men have borne themselves with a moderation and long-suffering patience that is a pattern for men and angels. It is greatly to be regretted that those abroad who influence public opinion sometimes represent that we do not mean what we say, that our object through all is to manufacture electioneering capital. Nothing could be more incorrect. Our domestic and foreign affairs are as distinct as an honest man keeps his personal and his trust funds. Outside our boundaries we know no parties, but are, in the words of one who will be remembered, " AMERICANS ALL."

APPENDIX A.

EFFECT OF THE INFLUX OF THE PRECIOUS METALS.

BUT if this is true, America was from another point of view highly detrimental to our material interests, annihilating the national industry and commerce, through the want of wise direction, and rendering us poor in the midst of abundance. The Spaniards, believing that a nation is rich in proportion to the amount of the precious metals it possesses, applied restrictive legislation to gold and silver, and by preventing them from leaving the country reduced their' value as a medium of exchange, while everything rose in price. Industrial activity ceased in Spain; agriculture and commerce were abandoned; the only ambition was for the acquisition of the precious metals, and it did not occur to anyone that the products of the arts and of agriculture could be converted into money by exchange. The result was that whereas a million pounds of silk had been produced by some 6000 spindles in Granada at the beginning of the sixteenth century, the output was only 200,000 at the middle of the seventeenth; and that Toledo, in 12 years from 1663 to 1675, lost 8161 looms out of 15,000, which formerly supported 130,000 operatives.

At the same time foreigners, stimulated by the prospect of the precious metals of Spain, were developing their industries with prodigious rapidity, sending us their products either through the customhouse or by smuggling. Added to these were the franchises granted to their citizens by Genoa, Milan, Naples, and Holland; and our industries, not being able to produce anything at the same price and equal in quality, kept falling behind. The trade with the colonies might have been capable of maintaining the economic prosperity of Spain, but, subjected to an unwise system, it too yielded no beneficial results. Consequently the great cargoes of gold and silver that came were for the benefit of the foreigner, verifying the saying that the treasures of America formed a copious river which passed over a single aqueduct, and that aqueduct was Spain. If we desire to satisfy ourselves on this point, we may bear in mind that the metallic circulation of Europe before the discovery of America did not exceed $850,000,000, according to Jacob. The stock of the metals drawn from the new world in the first century amounted to 3,500,000,000 and to 8,500,000,000 in the second. This increase of money, without counting the precious metals that came indirectly as jewelry, reached Spain, and supplied the want of our domestic products, which we then began to procure outside of the kingdom instead of producing them at home.—*Orodea, "Historia de España," 2a edición, Valladolid, 1869, pp. 296--97.*

APPENDIX B.

MR. FISH TO MR. CUSHING.

No. 266.   DEPARTMENT OF STATE,
                            WASHINGTON, November 5, 1875.

WHILE remembering and observing the duties which this Government, as one of the family of nations, owes to another member, by public law, treaties, or the particular statutes of the United States, it would be idle to attempt to conceal the interest and sympathy with which Americans in the United States regard any attempt of a numerous people on this continent to be relieved of ties which hold them in the position of colonial subjection to a distant power, and to assume the independence and right of self-control which natural rights and the spirit of the age accord to them.

When, moreover, this struggle, in progress on our very borders, from its commencement has involved the property and interests of citizens of the United States, has disturbed our tranquillity and commerce, has called upon us not infrequently to witness barbarous violations of the rules of civilized warfare, and compelled us for the sake of humanity to raise our voice by way of protest; and when, more than all, we see in the contest the final struggle in this hemisphere between slavery and freedom, it would be strange indeed if the Government and people of this country failed at any time to take peculiar interest in the termination of such contest.

In this early instruction was expressed the sincere and unselfish hope of the President that the Government of Spain would seek some honorable and satisfactory adjustment, based upon emancipation and self-government, which would restore peace and afford a prospect of a return of prosperity to Cuba.

Almost two years have passed since those instructions were issued and those strong hopes expressed, and it would appear that the situation has in no respect improved.

The horrors of war have in no perceptible measure abated; the inconveniences and injuries which we then suffered have remained, and others have been added; the ravages of war have touched new parts of the island, and well-nigh ruined its financial and agricultural system and its relations to the commerce of the world. No effective steps have been taken to establish reforms or remedy abuses, and the effort to suppress the insurrection by force alone has been a complete failure.

In the mean time the material interests of trade and of commerce are impaired to a degree which calls for remonstrance, if not for another line of conduct, on the part of all commercial nations.

Whether it be from the severity and inhumanity with which the effort has been made to suppress the insurrection, and from a supposed justification of retaliation for violations of the rules of civilized warfare by other violations and by acts of barbarism, of incendiarism, and outrage, the world is witnessing on the part of the insurgents, whom Spain still claims as subjects, and for whose acts, if subjects, Spain must be held accountable in the judgment of the world, a warfare, not of the legitimate strife of relative force and strength, but of pillage and incendiarism, the burning of estates and of sugar mills, the destruction of the means of production and of the wealth of the island.

The United States purchases more largely than any other people of the productions of the island of Cuba, and therefore, more than any other for this reason, and still more by reason of its immediate neighborhood, is interested in the arrest of a system of wanton destruction which disgraces the age and affects every commercial people on the face of the globe.

Under these circumstances, and in view of the fact that Spain has rejected all suggestions of reform or offers of mediation made by this Government, and has refused all measures looking to a reconciliation, except on terms which make reconciliation an impossibility, the difficulty of the situation becomes increased.

When, however, in addition to these general causes of difficulty, we find the Spanish Government neglectful also of the obligations of treaties and solemn compacts, and unwilling to afford any redress for long-continued and well-founded wrongs suffered by our citizens, it becomes a serious question how long such a condition of things can or should be allowed to exist, and compels us to inquire whether the point has not been reached where longer endurance ceases to be possible.

During all this time, and under these aggravated circumstances, this Government has not failed to perform her obligations to Spain as scrupulously as toward other nations.

In fact, it might be said that we have not only been long-suffering, because of the embarassments surrounding the Spanish Government, but particularly careful to give no occasion for complaint for the same reason.

I regret to say that the authorities of Spain have not at all times appreciated our intentions or our purposes in these respects, and, while insisting that a state of war does not exist in Cuba and that no rights as belligerents should be accorded to the insurrectionists, have at the same time demanded for themselves all the rights and privileges which flow from actual and acknowledged war.

It will be apparent that such a state of things cannot continue. It is absolutely necessary to the maintenance of our relations with Spain, even on their present footing, that our just demands for the return to citizens of the United States of their estates in Cuba, unincumbered, and for securing to them a trial for offenses according to treaty provisions, and all other rights guaranteed by treaty and by public law, should be complied with.

Whether the Spanish Government, appreciating the forbearance of this country, will speedily and satisfactorily adjust the pending questions, not by the issue of empty orders or decrees without force or effect in Cuba, but by comprehensive and firm measures which shall everywhere be respected, I anxiously await further intelligence.

Moreover, apart from these particular questions, in the opinion of the President, the time has arrived when the interests of this country, the preservation of its commerce, and the instincts of humanity alike demand that some speedy and satisfactory ending be made of the strife that is devastating Cuba.

A disastrous conflict of more than seven years' duration has demonstrated the inability of Spain to maintain peace and order in an island lying at our door. Desolation and destruction of life and property have been the only results of this conflict.

The United States sympathizes in the fact that this inability results in a large degree from the unhappy condition of Spain at home, and to some extent from the distractions which are dividing her people. But the fact remains. Added to this are the large expanse of ocean separating the peninsula from the island and the want of harmony and of personal sympathy between the inhabitants of the territory of the home Government and those of the colony, the distinction of classes in the latter between rulers and subjects, the want of adaptation of the ancient colonial system of Spain to the present times, and to the ideas which the events of the past age have impressed upon the peoples of every reading and thinking country.

Great Britain, wisely, has relaxed the old system of colonial dependence, and is reaping the benefits in the contentedness and peaceful prosecution of the arts of peace and in the channels of commerce and industry, in colonies which under restraint might have questioned and resisted the power of control from a distant government and might have exhibited, as does Cuba, a chronic condition of insurrection, turbulence, and rebellion.

In addition to all this, it cannot be questioned that the continued maintenance, in the face of decrees and enactments to the contrary, of a compulsory system of slave labor is the cause of disquiet and of excitement to a large class in the island, as also in the United States, which the Government of Spain has led us, by very distinct assurances, to expect should be removed, and which the enlightened Christianity of the age condemns.

The contest and disorder in Cuba affect the United States directly and injuriously by the presence in this country of partisans of the revolt who have fled hither (in consequence of the proximity of territory) as to a political asylum, and who, by their plottings, are disturbers of the public peace.

The United States has exerted itself to the utmost, for seven years, to repress unlawful acts on the part of these self-exiled subjects of Spain, relying on the promise of Spain to pacify the island. Seven years of strain on the powers of this Government to fulfill all that the most exacting demands of one government can make, under any doctrine or claim of international obligation, upon another, have not witnessed the much hoped for pacification. The United States feels itself entitled to be relieved of this strain.

The severe measures, injurious to the United States and often in conflict with public law, which the colonial officers have taken to subdue the insurrection; the indifference, and ofttimes the offensive assaults upon the just susceptibilities of the people of the United States and their Government, which have characterized that portion of the peninsular population of Habana which has sustained and upheld, if it has not controlled, successive governors general, and which have led to the disregard of orders and decrees which the more enlarged wisdom and the more friendly councils of the home government had enacted; the cruelty and inhumanity which have characterized the contests, both on the part of the colonial government and of the revolt, for seven years, and the destruction of valuable properties and industries by arson and pillage, which Spain appears unable, however desirous, to prevent and stop, in an island three thousand miles distant from her shores, but lying within sight of our coast, with which trade and constant intercourse are unavoidable, are causes of annoyance and of injury to the United States, which a people cannot be expected to tolerate without the assured prospect of their termination.

The United States has more than once been solicited by the insurgents to extend to them its aid, but has for years hitherto resisted such solicitation, and has endeavored by the tender of its good offices, in the way of mediation, advice, and remonstrance to bring to an end a great evil, which has pressed sorely upon the interests both of the Government and of the people of the United States, as also upon the commercial interests of other nations.

A sincere friendship for Spain, and for her people, whether peninsular or insular, and an equally sincere reluctance to adopt any measures which might injure or humble the ancient ally of the United States, has characterized the conduct of this Government in every step during these sad and distressing years, and the President is still animated by the same feelings, and desires above all things to aid her and her people to enter once more upon the path of safety and repose.

It will be remembered that the President, in the year 1869, tendered the good offices of the United States for the purpose of bringing to a close the civil war in Cuba. This offer was made delicately, in good faith, and in friendship to both parties to the contest.

General Prim, as the representative of the Spanish Government, while recognizing the good faith and friendship with which this offer was made, replied:

We can better proceed in the present situation of things without even this friendly intervention. A time will come when the good offices of the United States will not be only useful but indispensable, in the final arrangements between Spain and Cuba. We will ascertain the form in which they can be employed and confidently count upon your assistance.

The United States replied that its good offices for that object would be at any time at the service of the parties to the conflict. This Government has ever since been ready thus to aid in restoring peace and quiet.

The Government of the United States has heretofore given expression to no policy in reference to the insurrection in Cuba, because it has honestly and sincerely hoped that no declaration of policy on its part would be required,

The President feels that longer reticence would be inconsistent with the interests of both Governments.

Our relations with Spain are in that critical position that another seizure similar to that of the *Virginius*, other executions of citizens of the United States in Cuba, other wrongs of a less objectionable character even than many which have been already suffered by our citizens with simple remonstrance, or possibly even some new act of exceptional severity in Cuba, may suddenly produce a feeling and excitement which might force events which this Government anxiously desires to avoid.

The President hopes that Spain may spontaneously adopt measures looking to a reconciliation, and to the speedy restoration of peace, and the organization of a stable and satisfactory system of government in the island of Cuba.

In the absence of any prospect of a termination of the war, or of any change in the manner in which it has been conducted on either side, he feels that the time is at hand when it may be the duty of other governments to intervene, solely with the view of bringing to an end a disastrous and destructive conflict, and of restoring peace in the island of Cuba. No government is more deeply interested in the order and peaceful administration of this island than is that of the United States, and none has suffered as has the United States from the condition which has obtained there during the past six or seven years. He will, therefore, feel it his duty at an early day to submit the subject in this light, and accompanied by an expression of the views above presented, for the consideration of Congress.

This conclusion is reached with reluctance and regret.

It is reached after every other expedient has been attempted and proved a failure, and in the firm conviction that the period has at last arrived when no other course remains for this Government.

It is believed to be a just and friendly act to frankly communicate this conclusion to the Spanish Government.

You will, therefore, take an early occasion thus to inform that Government.

In making the communication it is the earnest desire of the President to impress upon the authorities of Spain the continued friendly disposition of this Government, and that it has no ulterior or selfish objects in view, and no desire to become a party in the conflict, but is moved solely by the imperative necessities of a proper regard to its own protection and its own interests and the interests of humanity, and, as we firmly believe, in the ultimate interest of Spain itself.

In informing the Spanish Government of these conclusions pursuant hereto, you are authorized to read this instruction to the Minister of State or to state the substance and purport thereof, as you may deem most advisable.

You will, of course, keep me advised, by telegraph and by post, of your proceedings pursuant to this instruction.

I am, etc.,

HAMILTON FISH.

CALEB CUSHING, ESQ.,
Etc., etc., etc.

APPENDIX C.

(Portion relating to Cuba.)

THE past year has furnished no evidence of an approaching termination of the ruinous conflict which has been raging for seven years in the neighboring Island of Cuba. The same disregard of the laws of civilized warfare and of the just demands of humanity, which has heretofore called forth expressions of condemnation from the nations of Christendom, has continued to blacken the sad scene. Desolation, ruin, and pillage are pervading the rich fields of one of the most fertile and productive regions of the earth, and the incendiary's torch, firing plantations and valuable factories and buildings, is the agent marking the alternate advance or retreat of contending parties.

The protracted continuance of this strife seriously affects the interests of all commercial nations, but those of the United States more than others, by reason of close proximity, its larger trade and intercourse with Cuba, and the fre-

quent and intimate personal and social relations
which have grown up between its citizens and
those of the island. Moreover the property of
our citizens in Cuba is large, and is rendered
insecure and depreciated in value and in capacity
of production by the continuance of the strife
and the unnatural mode of its conduct. The
same is true, differing only in degree, with respect to the interests and people of other nations;
and the absence of any reasonable assurance of
a near termination of the conflict must, of
necessity, soon compel the states thus suffering
to consider what the interests of their own
people and their duty toward themselves may
demand.

I have hoped that Spain would be enabled to
establish peace in her colony, to afford security
to the property and the interests of our citizens,
and allow legitimate scope to trade and commerce and the natural productions of the
island. Because of this hope, and from an extreme reluctance to interfere in the most remote
manner in the affairs of another and a friendly
nation, especially of one whose sympathy and
friendship in the struggling infancy of our own
existence must ever be remembered with grati-
tude, I have patiently and anxiously waited
the progress of events. Our own civil conflict
is too recent for us not to consider the difficulties which surround a government distracted by
a dynastic rebellion at home, at the same time
that it has to cope with a separate insurrection

in a distant colony. But, whatever causes may have produced the situation which so grievously affects our interests, it exists, with all its attendant evils, operating directly upon this country and its people. Thus far all the efforts of Spain have proved abortive, and time has marked no improvement in the situation. The armed bands of either side now occupy nearly the same ground as in the past, with the difference, from time to time, of more lives sacrificed, more property destroyed, and wider extents of fertile and productive fields and more and more of valuable property constantly wantonly sacrificed to the incendiary's torch.

In contests of this nature, where a considerable body of people who have attempted to free themselves of the control of the superior government have reached such point in occupation of territory, in power, and in general organization as to constitute in fact a body politic; having a government in substance as well as in name; possessed of the elements of stability, and equipped with the machinery for the administration of internal policy and the execution of its laws; prepared and able to administer justice at home as well as in its dealings with other powers, it is within the province of those other powers to recognize its existence as a new and independent nation. In such cases other nations simply deal with an actually existing condition of things, and recognize as one of the powers of the earth that body politic which, possessing the necessary elements, has, in fact, become a new power; in a word the creation of a new State is a fact.

To establish the condition of things essential to the recognition of this fact, there must be a people occupying a known territory, united under some known and defined form of government, acknowledged by those subject thereto, in which the functions of government are administered by usual methods, competent to mete out justice to citizens and strangers, to afford remedies for public and for private wrongs, and able to assume the correlative international obligations and capable of performing the corresponding international duties resulting from its acquisition of the rights of sovereignty. A power should exist, complete in its organization, ready to take and able to maintain its place among the nations of the earth.

While conscious that the insurrection in Cuba has shown a strength and endurance which make it at least doubtful whether it be in the power of Spain to subdue it, it seems unquestionable that no such civil organization exists which may be recognized as an independent government, capable of performing its international obligations and entitled to be treated as one of the powers of the earth. A recognition under such circumstances would be inconsistent with the facts, and would compel the power granting it soon to support by force the government to which it had really given its only claim of existence. In my judgment, the United States should adhere to the policy and the principles which have heretofore been its sure and safe guides in like contests between revolted colonies and their mother country, and, acting only upon the clearest evidence, should avoid any possibility of suspicion or of imputation.

A recognition of the independence of Cuba being in my opinion impracticable and indefensible, the question which next presents itself is that of the recognition of belligerent rights in the parties to the contest.

In a former message to Congress I had occasion to consider this question, and reached the conclusion that the conflict in Cuba, dreadful and devastating as were its incidents, did not rise to the fearful dignity of war. Regarding it now, after this lapse of time, I am unable to see that any notable success or any marked or real advance on the part of the insurgents has essentially changed the character of the contest. It has acquired greater age, but not greater or more formidable proportions. It is possible that the acts of foreign powers, and even acts of Spain herself, of this very nature might be pointed to in defense of such recognition. But now, as in its past history, the United States should carefully avoid the false lights which might lead it into the mazes of doubtful law and of questionable propriety, and adhere rigidly and sternly to the rule which has been its guide, of doing only that which is right and honest and of good

report. The question of according or withhold-
ing rights of belligerency must be judged in
every case in view of the particular attending
facts. Unless justified by necessity, it is always
and justly regarded as an unfriendly act and a
gratuitous demonstration of moral support to
the rebellion. It is necessary and it is required
when the interests and rights of another government or of its people are so far affected
by a pending civil conflict as to require a definition of its relations to the parties thereto.
But this conflict must be one which will be
recognized in the sense of international law as
war. Belligerence, too, is a fact. The mere existence of contending armed bodies, and their
occasional conflicts, do not constitute war in the
sense referred to.

Applying to the existing condition of affairs
in Cuba the test recognized by publicists and
writers on international law, and which have
been observed by nations of dignity, honesty,
and power, when free from sensitive or selfish
and unworthy motives, I fail to find in the insurrection the existence of such a substantial political organization, real, palpable, and manifest to
the world, having the forms and capable of the
ordinary functions of government toward its own
people and to other States, with courts for the
administration of justice, with a local habitation,
possessing such organization of force, such material, such occupation of territory, as to take the
contest out of the category of a mere rebellious

insurrection, or occasional skirmish, and place it on the terrible footing of war, to which a recognition of belligerency would aim to elevate it. The contest, moreover, is solely on land; the insurrection has not possessed itself of a single seaport whence it may send forth its flag, nor has it any means of communication with foreign powers except through the military lines of its adversaries. No apprehension of any of those sudden and difficult complications which a war upon the ocean is apt to precipitate upon the vessels, both commercial and national, and upon the consular officers of other powers, calls for the definition of their relations to the parties to the contest.

Considered as a question of expediency, I regard the accordance of belligerent rights still to be as unwise and premature as I regard it to be at present indefensible as a measure of right. Such recognition entails upon the country according the rights which flow from it difficult and complicated duties, and requires the exaction from the contending parties of the strict observance of their rights and obligations. It confers the right of search upon the high seas by vessels of both parties; it would subject the carrying of arms and munitions of war, which now may be transported freely and without interruption in the vessels of the United States, to detention and possible seizure; it would give rise to countless vexatious questions; would release the parent government from responsibility for acts done by the insurgents, and would invest Spain with the right to exercise the supervision recognized by our treaty of 1795 over our commerce on the high seas; a very large part of which, in its traffic between the Atlantic and the Gulf States and between all of them and the States on the Pacific, passes through the waters which wash the shores of Cuba. The exercise of this supervision could scarce fail to lead, if not to abuses, certainly to collisions perilous to the peaceful relations of the two States. There can be little doubt as to what result such supervision would, before long, draw this nation. It would be unworthy of the United States to inaugurate the possibilities of such result by measures of questionable right or expediency or by any indirection. Apart from any question of theoretical right, I am satisfied that while the accordance of belligerent rights to the insurgents in Cuba might give them a hope and an inducement to protract the struggle, it would be but a delusive hope and would not remove the evils which this government and its people are experiencing, but would draw the United States into complications which it has waited long and already suffered much to avoid. The recognition of independence or of belligerency being thus, in my judgment, equally inadmissible, it remains to consider what course shall be adopted should the conflict not soon be brought to an end by acts of the parties themselves, and should the evils which result therefrom, affecting all nations, and particularly the United States, continue.

In such event I am of the opinion that other nations will be compelled to assume the responsibility which devolves upon them, and to seriously consider the only remaining measures possible, mediation and intervention. Owing perhaps to the large expanse of water separating the island from the peninsula, the want of harmony and of personal sympathy between the inhabitants of the colony and those sent thither to rule them, and want of adaptation of the ancient colonial system of Europe to the present times and to the ideas which the events of the past century have developed, the contending parties appear to have within themselves no depository of common confidence to suggest wisdom when passion and excitement have their sway, and to assume the part of peacemaker. In this view, in the earlier days of the contest, the good offices of the United States as a mediator were tendered in good faith, without any selfish purpose, in the interest of humanity and in sincere friendship for both parties, but were at the time declined by Spain, with the declaration, nevertheless, that at a future time they would be indispensable. No intimation has been received that, in the opinion of Spain, that time has been reached. And yet the strife continues, with all its dread horrors and all its injuries to the interests of the United States and of other nations. Each party seems quite capable of working

great injury and damage to the other, as well as
to all the relations and interests dependent on
the existence of peace in the island; but they
seem incapable of reaching any adjustment, and
both have thus far failed of achieving any success whereby one party shall possess and control the island to the exclusion of the other.
Under these circumstances the agency of others,
either by mediation or by intervention, seems to
be the only alternative which must sooner or
later be invoked for the termination of the strife.
At the same time, while thus impressed, I do not
at this time recommend the adoption of any
measure of intervention. I shall be ready at all
times, and as the equal friend of both parties, to
respond to a suggestion that the good offices
of the United States will be acceptable to aid in
bringing about peace honorable to both.

It is due to Spain, so far as this Government is
concerned, that the agency of a third power, to
which I have adverted, shall be adopted only as
a last expedient. Had it been the desire of the
United States to interfere in the affairs of Cuba,
repeated opportunities for so doing have been
presented within the last few years; but we have
remained passive, and have performed our whole
duty and all international obligations to Spain
with friendship, fairness, and fidelity, and with a
spirit of patience and forbearance which nega-
tives every possible suggestion of desire to interfere or to add to the difficulties with which she
has been surrounded. The Government of

Spain has recently submitted to our Minister at Madrid certain proposals which it is hoped may be found to be the basis if not the actual submission of terms to meet the requirements of the particular griefs of which this Government has felt itself entitled to complain. These proposals have not yet reached me in their full text. On their arrival they will be taken into careful examination, and may, I hope, lead to satisfactory adjustment of the questions to which they refer, and remove the possibility of future occurrences such as have given rise to our just complaints. It is understood, also, that renewed efforts are being made to introduce reforms in the internal administration of the island. Persuaded, however, that a proper regard for the interests of the United States and of its citizens entitle it to relief from the strain to which it has been subjected by the difficulties of the questions and the wrongs and losses which arise from the contest in Cuba, and that the interests of humanity itself demand the cessation of the strife before the whole island shall be laid waste and larger sacrifices of life be made, I shall feel it my duty, should my hopes of a satisfactory adjustment and of the early restoration of peace and the removal of future causes of complaint be unhappily disappointed, to make a further communication to Congress at some period not far remote, and, during the present session, recommending what may then seem to me to be necessary.

APPENDIX D.

CAPITULACIÓN DEL ZANJON.

ARTÍCULO I.   Concesión á la Isla de Cuba de las mismas condiciones políticas, orgánicas y administrativas de que disfruta la Isla de Puerto Rico.

ART°. II.   Olvido de lo pasado respecto de los delitos políticos cometidos desde el año de 1868 hasta el presente, y libertad de los encausados ó que se hallen cumpliendo condena dentro y fuera de la Isla.   Indulto general á los desertores del Ejército español sin distinción de nacionalidad, haciendo extensiva esta cláusula á cuantos hubiesen tomada parte directa ó indirectamente en el movimiento revolucionario.

ART°. III.   Libertad á los esclavos y colonos asiáticos que se hallen hoy en las filas insurrectas.

ART°. IV.   Ningún individuo que, en virtud de esta capitulación, reconozca y quede bajo la acción del Gobierno español podrá ser compelido á prestar ningún servicio de guerra mientras no se establezca la paz.

ART°. V.   Todo individuo que desee marchar fuera de la Isla, queda facultado, y se le proporcionarán por el Gobierno español los medios de hacerlo, sin tocar en población si así lo deseare.

Art°. VI. La capitulación de cada fuerza se efectuará en despoblado, donde con antelación se depositarán las armas y demás elementos de guerra.

Art°. VII. El General en Jefe del Ejército español, á fin de facilitar los medios de que puedan avenirse los Departamentos, franqueará todas las vías de mar y tierra de que pueda disponer.

Art°. VIII. Considerar lo pactado con el Comité del Centro como general y sin restricciones particulares para todos los Departamentos de la Isla que acepten estas proposiciones.

El Zanjón, 10 de febrero de 1878.

(Translation.)

CAPITULATION OF EL ZANJÓN.

Article I. Concession to the island of Cuba of the same political privileges, organic and administrative, enjoyed by the island of Puerto Rico.*

Art. II. Oblivion of the past, as regards political offenses committed since the year 1868 up to the present; and liberty to those who are under trial or are fulfilling sentences within or

* This merely means that Cuba should be allowed representation in the Spanish Cortes. That was then the organic difference between the two islands. But see p. 183.

outside of the island. A general pardon to the deserters from the Spanish army, without distinction of nativity; this clause to be extended to all those who have taken any part, directly or indirectly, in the revolutionary movement.

ART. III. Freedom to the slaves and Asiatic colonists now in the insurrectionary ranks.

ART. IV. No person who in virtue of this capitulation recognizes and remains within the authority of the Spanish Government shall be compelled to render any military service until peace is established.

ART. V. Every person who desires to leave the island shall be at liberty to do so, and he shall be furnished by the Spanish Government with the means therefor, without entering a town, if he should so desire.

ART. VI. The capitulation of each force shall take place outside the towns, and the arms and implements of war shall be primarily laid down there.

ART. VII. The general in chief of the Spanish army, in order to facilitate the means for uniting the other departments in this convention, shall make free all the means of communication, by sea and land, that he can dispose of.

ART. VIII. The Agreement made with the Central Committee shall be considered as general, and without special restrictions, for all the departments of the island which accept these propositions.

EL ZANJON, February 10, 1878.

APPENDIX E.

ARTICLES OF PACIFICATION WITH THE MAROONS
OF TRELAWNEY TOWN, CONCLUDED MARCH
1, 1738.

IN the name of God, Amen. Whereas Captain Cudjoe, Captain Accompong, Captain Johnny, Captain Cuffee, Captain Quaco, and several other negroes, their dependents and adherents, have been in a state of war and hostility, for several years past, against our sovereign lord the King, and the inhabitants of this island; and whereas peace and friendship among mankind, and the preventing the effusion of blood, is agreeable to God, consonant to reason, and desired by every good man; and whereas his Majesty, King George the Second, King of Great Britain, France, and Ireland, of Jamaica Lord, Defender of the Faith, etc., has, by his letters patent, dated February the twenty-fourth, one thousand and seven hundred and thirty-eight, in the twelfth year of his reign, granted full power and authority to John Guthrie and Francis Sadler, Esquires, to negotiate and conclude a treaty of peace and friendship with the aforesaid Captain Cudjoe, and the rest of his captains, adherents, and others his men; they mutually, sincerely, and amicably have agreed:

I.   That all hostilities shall cease on both sides forever.

II.   That the said Captain Cudjoe, the rest of his captains, adherents, and men, shall be forever hereafter in a perfect state of freedom and liberty, excepting those who have been taken by them, or fled to them, within two years last past, if such are willing to return to their said masters and owners, with full pardon and indemnity from their said masters and owners for what is past; provided always, that, if they are not willing to return, they shall remain in subjection to Captain Cudjoe and in friendship with us, according to the form and tenor of this treaty.

III.   That they shall enjoy and possess, for themselves and posterity forever, all the lands situate and lying between Trelawney Town and the Cockpits, to the amount of fifteen hundred acres, bearing northwest from the said Trelawney Town.

IV.   That they shall have liberty to plant the said lands with coffee, cocoa, ginger, tobacco, and cotton, and to breed cattle, hogs, goats, or any other stock, and dispose of the produce or increase of the said commodities to the inhabitants of this island; próvided always, that when they bring the said commodities to market, they shall apply first to the custos, or any other magistrate of the respective parishes where they expose their goods to sale, for a license to vend the same.

V. That Captain Cudjoe, and all the captains, adherents, and people now in subjection to him, shall all live together within the bounds of Trelawney Town, and that they have the liberty to hunt where they shall think fit, except within three miles of any settlement, crawl, or pen; provided always, that in case the hunters of Captain Cudjoe and those of the other settlements meet, then the hogs to be equally divided between both parties.

VI. That the said Captain Cudjoe, and his successors, do use their best endeavors to take, kill, suppress, or destroy, either by themselves, or jointly with any other number of men, commanded on that service by his Excellency the Governor, or commander in chief for the time being, all rebels wheresoever they be, throughout this island, unless they submit to the same terms of accommodation granted to Captain Cudjoe, and his successors.

VII. That in case this island be invaded by any foreign enemy, the said Captain Cudjoe, and his successors hereinafter named or to be appointed, shall then, upon notice given, immediately repair to any place the Governor for the time being shall appoint, in order to repel the said invaders with his or their utmost force, and to submit to the orders of the commander in chief on that occasion.

VIII. That if any white man shall do any

manner of injury to Captain Cudjoe, his successors, or any of his or their people, they shall apply to any commanding officer or magistrate in the neighborhood for justice; and in the case Captain Cudjoe, or any of his people, shall do any injury to any white person, he shall submit himself, or deliver up such offender to justice.

IX.   That if any negroes shall hereafter run away from their masters or owners, and fall into Captain Cudjoe's hands, they shall be immediately sent back to the chief magistrate of the next parish where they are taken; and those that bring them are to be satisfied for their trouble, as the legislature shall appoint.

X.   That all negroes taken, since the raising of this party by Captain Cudjoe's people, shall immediately be returned.

XI.   That Captain Cudjoe, and his successors, shall wait on his Excellency, or the commander in chief for the time being, every year, if thereunto required.

XII.   That Captain Cudjoe, during his life, and the captains succeeding him, shall have full power to inflict any punishment they think proper for crimes committed by their men among themselves, death only excepted; in which case, if the Captain thinks they deserve death, he shall be obliged to bring them before any justice of the peace, who shall order proceedings on their trial equal to those of other free negroes.

XIII.   That Captain Cudjoe, with his people,

shall cut, clear, and keep open, large and convenient roads from Trelawney Town to Westmoreland and St. James', and, if possible, to St. Elizabeth's.

XIV. That two white men, to be nominated by his Excellency, or the commander in chief for the time being, shall constantly live and reside with Captain Cudjoe and his successors, in order to maintain a friendly correspondence with the inhabitants of this island.

XV. That Captain Cudjoe shall, during his life, be chief commander in Trelawney Town; after his decease the command to devolve on his brother, Captain Accompong; and in case of his decease, on his next brother, Captain Johnny; and, failing him, Captain Cuffee shall succeed; who is to be succeeded by Captain Quaco; and after all their demises, the Governor, or commander in chief for the time being, shall appoint, from time to time, whom he thinks fit for that command.

APPENDIX F.

INTERNATIONAL law, or the law of nations, is
a body of rules and principles which have
grown up by the general consent of civilized
nations, regulating their treatment of each other.
Its foundation is the general good of mankind;
its sanctions are common consent, a recognition
of its justice, and a fear of general retaliation; its
standards of authority are the decisions of regularly organized prize courts and the compilations
of eminent publicists whose learning, wisdom,
and fairness are generally recognized. Rules of
international law are sometimes expressly recognized, or modified, by treaties; but these treaties
are binding only on their signatories.

Every nation has a right, under the direction
of its supreme head, to make war upon any other
nation to secure a right or prevent a wrong; and

* The references to sections are to those of Wheaton's
" Elements of International Law," eighth edition, with notes
by Richard Henry Dana, Jr., LL. D.

it is allowed to be its own judge of the right or wrong.

The parties to a war are called *belligerents;* and to each other they are mutually *enemies.* The term *enemy* applies to all the persons of the opposite nation. All who are not involved in any way in the war are *neutrals.* A neutral may take part on either side and thus become the *ally* of one belligerent and the *enemy* of the other.

Every belligerent claims that his side of the quarrel is just; and a neutral has no right to judge between them, so as to take any action on such judgment. His duty is to treat both precisely alike, so far as the war is concerned; which can only be done by letting them entirely alone, offering no hindrances or facilities to either.

A declaration of war is not essential,* but is a convenience to neutrals, that they may be quickly and definitely informed of the fact.

A belligerent has a right to use all the force necessary to bring his enemy to his terms; but he is not justified in inflicting unnecessary pain or damage. He may kill his enemy, but only when the latter is in the performance of some hostile act, including the attempt to escape out of captivity. He may not kill in a cruel or un-

---

*Brevet Lieutenant Colonel J. F. Maurice, R. A., in his work entitled " Hostilities without Declaration of War,") published by the Intelligence Division of the British War Office), enumerates 103 cases, from 1700 to 1870, of hostilities occurring between civilized powers prior to any declaration or warning.

usual manner. The old rule that permitted the captor to kill prisoners that he had not the means of keeping would now be abhorrent to humanity. The right to hold prisoners is only commensurate with the power.

A belligerent has a right to take or destroy the enemy's property wherever he can; but, as he cannot enter a neutral jurisdiction to do this, he is limited to his own country, the enemy's country, unclaimed islands, and the open seas— practically, the second and fourth of these. But it is the most approved practice of civilized nations to spare all persons and property on land that are not either impeding their operations or contributing to those of the enemy, or are neces- sary to self-preservation. The enemy's ships and goods found on the high seas are lawful prize; but must first be submitted to the judg- ment of a prize court to determine the legal right. It cannot be a court of the enemy, and neutrals generally refuse the use of theirs; hence it must be the court of the captor or his ally.

From time immemorial the goods of an enemy on board of a neutral ship are liable to seizure (Sec. 442). It is the interest of maritime nations, and those having large commerce and small navies, to restrict the right as much as possible. This can only be done by treaty. Many treaties, especially those of the United States, contain a provision that *free ships make free goods.* It is so provided in the treaty with Spain of October 27, 1795, Article XV.

On the converse, by the principles originally accepted, enemy's ships do not make enemy's goods; but, in many modern treaties and for sake of simplicity, the nationality of the ship is made to determine the character of the cargo (Sec. 454). Carrying enemy's goods does not work forfeiture of the ship.

The carrying of contraband of war forfeits the ship and cargo of the neutral carrier. By thus aiding directly in the war, he ceases to that extent to be neutral, and becomes an ally, and consequently an enemy. All articles *specially* adapted to the purposes of war are contraband. Artcles that minister only to the wants of women and children, to the offices of religion, the fine arts, education, and learning are not contraband. Between these are a vast number of articles that may or may not be contraband, according to circumstances. When destined for military or naval stations or forces they are contraband; if going to places not connected with warlike operations or preparations they are not. To prevent ambiguity, articles of contraband are enumerated by name in many modern treaties, as in that with Spain in 1795. Sometimes a clause is added that all articles not so named shall be free. A further clause is added in some treaties that the ship shall be exempt, especially when the ship and cargo have different owners

(Sec. 505).   If seized, she must be submitted to a prize court.

Contraband of war includes military—not civil—persons and dispatches (Sec. 502--503).

Siege is an attempt to capture a town or fort of the enemy; *blockade* an attempt to prevent anyone from going in or out.   An attempt to pass a blockading or besieging force forfeits ship and cargo.   But there are conditions.   The investing force must be such, and so placed, as to make it dangerous to pass.   The neutral must have due notice of the blockade.   Proclamation or rumor is not sufficient.   The neutral must be warned by the blockading squadron; or the fact of the blockade must be so well known in the place whence he comes that he cannot be supposed to be ignorant (Sec. 514).

To constitute a violation of blockade the cargo must have been taken on board after notice.   An innocent trader is to be warned off, but not allowed to enter.   A ship in the blockaded port must take in no more cargo after its commencement, but may pass out with what is already on board.

Neutral ships of war are not privileged to enter blockaded ports (Sec. 512, note).

The offense of carrying contraband or of violating blockade begins at the port of departure and continues throughout the voyage or until capture.   That of the blockade running covers the return homeward (Sec. 506).

A belligerent has the right to stop and search every peaceful ship that sails the sea. He needs to know whether she is an enemy, a bearer of enemy's goods, a bearer of contraband, or a blockade runner; and neither point can be determined without visit and search. This right, especially in the hands of rash and ignorant officers, is so vexatious that it is the interest of the rest of mankind that there should be no belligerents, or failing that, that their privileges should be as limited as possible. Hence the tendency of modern treaties.

A ship's papers, unless defective or fraudulent, are sufficient evidence of the character and destination of vessel and cargo. Usually they alone are examined.

The *public* vessels of a neutral are not liable to visitation and search.

A vessel chased at sea may not be followed within the limits of a neutral jurisdiction (Sec. 429).

The law of nations furnishes little or no guidance in the case where subjects rebel against their sovereign. An acknowledgment of belligerency by a neutral is a mere expression of opinion, but of an opinion unfavorable to the sovereign. It avails nothing unless followed by action. If the action be in aid of the sovereign the neutral becomes his ally, and the enemy of the rebels. If the action favors the rebels, the result is the reverse. In the latter case, the neutral has no right to complain if his vessels are searched at sea; but, by the act of search, the sovereign admits the belligerency.

A sovereign holds that those in revolt are enemies *de facto*, yet *de jure* subjects. He will bring them to their allegiance, if he can; if he cannot, they become independent, or parts of some other sovereignty. Such has been the history of America, North and South, for 130 years.

The fitting out of, or contributing to, expeditions against a sovereign or dependency is an unfriendly act, and may be a just cause of war. But the vigilance of the United States Government in preventing filibustering is based not so much on international law as upon express statute—the Act of April 20, 1818, which combines and enlarges several earlier acts.

M. M. R.

APPENDIX G.

BIBLIOGRAPHY.

F. D. Vives. Cuadro estadístico de la Isla de Cuba correspondiente al año 1827. Precedido de una descripción histórica, física, geográfica, y notas. Habana, 1829.

J. de la Pezuela. Ensayo histórico de la Isla de Cuba. Nueva York, 1842.

Bando de Gobernación y policía de la Isla de Cuba, expedido por el Excelentísimo Sr. D. Jerónimo Valdés, Presidente, Gobernador y Capitán General. Habana, 1842.

V. Vásquez Queipo. Informe sobre la población blanca en la Isla de Cuba. Madrid, 1845.

Ramón de la Sagra. Histórica física, política y natural de la Isla de Cuba. Publicada con real aprobación y bajo la protección de la Intendencia de la Habana. Madrid, 1849--61. 13 vols.

R. B. Kimball. Cuba and the Cubans; history and condition of the island. New York, 1850.

M. Torrente. Bosquejo económico-político de la Isla de Cuba. Madrid-Habana, 1852--53. 2 vols.

V. Feijoo Sotomayor. Isla de Cuba; inmigración de trabajadores españoles; documentos y memoria sobre esta materia. Habana, 1853.

José de la Concha. Memorias sobre el estado político, gobierno y administración de la Isla de Cuba. Madrid, 1853.

Llamamiento de la Isla de Cuba á la nación española. Por un hacendado. Nueva York, 1854.

P. A. Alfonso. Memorias de un Matancero. Apuntes para la historia de la Isla de Cuba con relación á la ciudad de San Carlos y San Severino de Matanzas. Matanzas, 1854.

Antonio Saco. Folletos escritos contra la anexión de la Isla de Cuba á los Estados Unidos de América. Nueva York, 1856.

Alexander von Humboldt. The Island of Cuba. Translated from the Spanish, with notes and a preliminary essay, by J. S. Thrasher. New York, 1856.

R. Pasarón y Lastra. La Isla de Cuba considerada económicamente. Madrid, 1858.

D. A. Galiano. Cuba en 1858. Madrid, 1859.

P. Santacilla. Lecciones orales sobre la historia de Cuba, pronunciadas en el Ateneo Democrático Cubano de Nueva York. Nueva Orleans, 1859.

J. F. Erenchun. Anales de la Isla de Cuba. Diccionario administrativo, económico, estadístico y legislativo. Madrid-Habana, 1857--64. 3 vols.

Jegor von Sivers. Cuba, die Perle der Antillen. Leipzig, 1861.

Ramón de la Sagra. Historia económico-política, intelectual y moral de la Isla de Cuba. Nueva edición. París, 1861.

J. de la Pezuela. Diccionario geográfico-estadístico de la Isla de Cuba. Madrid, 1863. 4 vols.

————. Necesidades de Cuba. Madrid, 1865.

Fernández de Castro. Estudios sobre las minas de oro en la Isla de Cuba. Habana, 1865.

Emilio Blanchet. Compendio de la historia de Cuba. Matanzas, 1866.

Céspedes y Orellano. Elementos teórico-prácticos de procedimientos civiles con aplicación á las islas de Cuba y Puerto Rico. 2a edición. Habana, 1866. 2 vols.

F. de Armas y Céspedes. De la esclavitud en Cuba. Madrid, 1866.

F. Figuera. Estudios sobre la Isla de Cuba. La cuestión social. Madrid, 1866.

Jacobo de la Pezuela. Historia de la guerra de Cuba. Madrid, 1868. 4 vols.

R. Ferrer. Estudios físicos, geográficos y geológicos de Cuba. (Pub. in *La Revista de España*, Tomo XXII, 1871).

J. Zaragoza. Las insurrecciones en Cuba. Apuntes para la historia política de esta isla en el presente siglo. Madrid, 1872--73. 2 vols.

S. Hazard. Cuba with Pen and Pencil. London, 1873.

A. Gallenga. The Pearl of the Antilles. London, 1873.

Miguel Blanco Herrero. La Isla de Cuba, su

situación actual y reformas que reclama. Madrid, 1876.

Hippolyte Piron. L'Ile de Cuba. Paris, 1876.

Los tres primeros historiadores de la Isla de Cuba. Reproducción de las historias de José Martín de Arrate y Antonio José Valdés, y publicación de la inédita de Ignacio de Urrutia y Montoya. Adicionado con notas y aumentado con la descripción histórica de las ciudades, etc., de esta isla. Habana, 1876--77. 3 vols.

Cándido Pieltáin, Capitán General. La Isla de Cuba desde mediados de abril á fines de octubre de 1873. Madrid, 1879.

Pedro Gutiérrez y Salazar. Reformas de Cuba; cuestión social. Madrid, 1879.

J. W. Steele. Cuban Sketches. New York, 1881.

———— The same. New, cheaper edition. New York, 1885.

M. M. Ballou. Due South; Cuba, Past and Present. Boston, 1885.

Rafael G. Eslava. Juicio crítico de Cuba en 1887. Habana, 1887.

Francisco Moreno. Cuba y su gente; apuntes para la historia. Madrid, 1887.

Raimundo Cabera. Cuba y sus jueces. (An answer to the foregoing). Habana, 1887.

Francisco Moreno. El país del chocolate; la inmoralidad en Cuba. Madrid, 1887.

Reseña geográfica y estadística de España. Por la Dirección general del Instituto Geográfico y Estadístico. Madrid, 1888. (Pp. 1051--65 relate to Cuba.)

Leopoldo Barrios y Carrión, Capitán de Estado Mayor. Sobre la historia de la guerra de Cuba. Barcelona, *Revista Científico-Militar,* 1888-90.

Rafael G. Eslava. Historia colonial de Cuba desde su descubrimiento hasta el año 1888. Habana, 1889.

F. A. Conte. La lucha política en Cuba (1878-89). Habana, 1889.

José M. de la Torre. Novísimos elementos de geografía é historia de la Isla de Cuba. Completamente reformada por José Imberno. Habana, 1889.

Elisée Reclus. The Earth and its Inhabitants. North America. Edited by A. H. Keane. New York, 1891. (Pp. 354-82 of vol ii. relate to Cuba.)

John C. Prince. Cuba Illustrated. Sixth edition. New York, 1893.

Eugenio Antonio Flores, oficial de Voluntarios. La guerra de Cuba; apuntes para la historia. Madrid, 1895.

Rafael Delforme Salto. Cuba y la reforma colonial en España. Madrid, 1895.

Antonio Perala. Anales de la guerra de Cuba. Madrid, 1896.

Beligerantes y neutrales; rebeldes y amigos. Estudios de derecho internacional público. Por un aficionado. Madrid, 1896.

Severo Gómez Núñez, Capitán de Artillería.

Estudios geográficos y estadísticos de la Isla de Cuba. (Author decorated for same.) Madrid, 1896.

Fernando López Tuero. Estudio moral de los factores de la producción en Cuba y Puerto Rico. Madrid, 1896.

Los Estados Unidos contra España. Por un optimista. Madrid, 1896.

Juan Calero y Ortega, Teniente de Infantería. Guerras irregulares y de montaña. (Author decorated for same.) Madrid, 1896.

Vicente Torres y González. La insurrección de Cuba. Madrid, 1896.

Bailly-Bailliere. Anuario del comercio, de la industria, de la magistratura y de la administración, ó directorio de las 400,000 señas de España, Ultramar, Estados Hispano-Americanos, y Portugal. Año xviii. Madrid, 1896. (Pp. 2414--2535, vol. ii., relate to Cuba.)

Raimundo Cabrera. Cuba and the Cubans. Translated from the eighth edition of "Cuba y sus jueces" [*vide supra*] by Laura Guiteras. Revised and edited by L. E. Levy, and completed with a supplementary appendix by the editor. Philadelphia, 1896.

Rafael M. Merchán. Cuba: justificación de su guerra de independencia. Bogotá, 1896.

España y Cuba. Estado político y administrativo de la Grande Antilla bajo la dominación española. Madrid, 1896.

Spanish Rule in Cuba; Laws Governing the

Island. (Abstract translation of the foregoing, with additional notes.) New York, 1896.

James Hyde Clark. Cuba and the Fight for Freedom. Philadelphia, 1896.

Murat Halstead. The Story of Cuba: Her Struggles for Liberty, the Cause, Crisis, and Destiny of the Pearl of the Antilles. Chicago, 1896.

Fidel G. Pierra. Cuba: Physical Features of Cuba, her Past, Present, and Possible Future. New York, 1896.

Cuban Belligerency: Petition of Tomás Estrada Palma, Delegate of the Republic of Cuba; Statement of the law, by Horatio S. Rubens, Counsel for the delegation. New York [1896].

Antonio Romero Torrado, Ex-Presidente de la Audiencia de la Habana. El problema de Cuba. Madrid, 1896.

Leandro González Alcosta. Qué pasa en Cuba; por qué crece la insurrección; y cómo se extravía aquí la opinión pública. 2a edición. León, 1896.

ANNOTATED TEXTS OF LAWS RELATING TO CUBA.

El procedimiento administrativo en los negocios de ultramar, organizado por real decreto de 21 de septiembre de 1888; y la ley de lo contencioso-administrativo, aplicada á las islas de

Cuba, Puerto Rico y Filipinas por real decreto de 23 de noviembre de 1888. Madrid, 1889.

Ley de enjuiciamiento criminal vigente en Cuba y Puerto Rico, anotada por la redacción de la *Revista de los Tribunales*. Madrid, 1889.

Compilación de las disposiciones orgánicas de la administración de justicia en las provincias de ultramar, precedida de una introducción histórica. Anotada y concordada con la legislación anterior y la de la Península, y con las leyes procesales, y seguida de varios apéndices. Madrid, 1891.

Código penal para las islas de Cuba y Puerto Rico, anotado con la jurisprudencia del tribunal supremo por D. Manuel Ochotorena. 2a edición. Madrid, 1894.

Ley de enjuiciamiento civil, reformada para las islas de Cuba y Puerto Rico. Aprobada el 25 de septiembre de 1885. Anotada con la jurisprudencia del tribunal supremo. 2a edición. Madrid, 1894.

LIST OF UNITED STATES EXECUTIVE DOCUMENTS RELATING TO CUBA.

Treaty between United States and Spain. Correspondence relative to the delays by the Governor and Captain General of the Island of Cuba. June 13, 1821. Senate Docs., No 2, 18th Cong., 2d sess.

Resolution on the Transfer of Cuba from

Spain. Representative Markley. April 7, 1826. H. R. Reports, No. 39, 19th Cong., 1st sess.

Resolution on Tonnage of Cuban Vessels. April 19, 1848. Senate Misc. Docs., No. 125, 30th Cong., 1st sess.

Message on Imprisonment of W. H. Bush by authorities of Cuba. President James K. Polk. Feb. 23, 1849. Senate Ex. Docs., No. 33, 30th Cong., 2d sess.

Proclamation on Invasion of Cuba. President Zachary Taylor. Dec. 4, 1849. Senate Ex. Docs., No. 1, 31st Cong., 1st sess.

Message on Cuban affairs. President Zachary Taylor. June 3, 1850. Senate Ex. Docs., No. 57, 31st Cong., 1st sess.

Proclamation on the Cuban Invasion. President Millard Fillmore. 1851. H. R. Ex. Docs., No. 2, 32d Cong., 1st sess.

Message on Prisoners Captured by Spanish Authorities. President Millard Fillmore. Feb. 27, 1851. Senate Ex. Docs., No. 41, 31st Cong., 2d sess.

Message on Foreigners in Cuban Expedition. President Millard Fillmore. July 2, 1852. H. R. Ex. Docs., No. 115, 32d Cong., 1st sess.

Message on the Island of Cuba. President Millard Fillmore. July 13, 1852. H. R. Docs., No. 121, 32d Cong., 1st sess.

Message Relative to a Proposed Tripartite Convention on the Subject of Cuba. President Millard Fillmore. Jan. 4, 1853. Senate Ex. Docs., No. 13, 32d Cong., 2d sess.

Resolutions on Case of James H. West, Imprisoned in Cuba. Rhode Island Legislature. March 9, 1853. Senate Misc. Docs., No. 2, 33d Cong., special sess.

Report on Seizure of the *Black Warrior* at Habana, Feb. 28, 1854. President Franklin Pierce. March 15, 1854. H. R. Ex. Docs., No. 76, 33d Cong., 1st sess.

Resolutions on Abolition of Slavery in Cuba. Louisiana Legislature, March 16, 1854. H. R. Misc. Docs., No. 79, 33d Cong., 1st sess.

Message on the Acquisition of Cuba. President James Buchanan. Jan. 19, 1859. Ex. Docs., No. 57, 35th Cong., 2d sess.

Report on the Acquisition of Cuba. Senator John Slidell. Jan. 24, 1859. Senate Reports, No. 351, 35th Cong., 2d sess.

Message on Imprisonment of American Citizens in Cuba. President James Buchanan. April 2, 1860. Ex. Docs., No. 54, 36th Cong., 1st sess.

Letter on Recognition of Cuba. Governor of South Carolina. Dec. 9, 1869. Senate Misc. Docs., No. 5, 41st Cong., 2d sess.

Message on Relations with Cuba. President U. S. Grant. Dec. 15, 1869. H. R. Ex. Docs., No. 22, 41st Cong., 2d sess.

Message on Murder of American Citizens in Cuba. President U. S. Grant. Feb. 18, 1870. H. R. Ex. Docs., No. 140, part 2, 41st Cong., 2d sess.

Message on Affairs in the Island of Cuba. President U. S. Grant. Feb. 22, 1870. H. R. Ex. Docs., No. 160, 41st Cong., 2d sess.

Resolution on Recognition of Cuba. Iowa Legislature. March 28, 1870. H. R. Misc. Docs., No. 103, 41st Cong., 2d sess.

Resolution on the Revolution in Cuba. Maryland Senate. April 11, 1870. H. R. Misc. Docs., No. 125, 41st Cong., 2d sess.

Message on the Insurrection in Cuba. President U. S. Grant. June 13, 1870. Senate Ex. Docs., No. 99, 41st Cong., 2d sess.

Message on Hostilities in Cuba. President U. S. Grant. July 9, 1870. Senate Ex. Docs., No. 108, 41st Cong., 2d sess.

Message on Emancipation in Cuba. President U. S. Grant. July 13, 1870. Senate Ex. Docs., No. 113, 41st Cong., 2d sess.

Message on Relations with Cuba. President U. S. Grant. Feb. 13, 1872. Senate Ex. Docs., No. 32, 42d Cong., 2d sess.

Resolution on Recognition of Cuba. Kansas Legislature. March 4, 1872. H. R. Misc. Docs., No. 101, 42d Cong., 2d sess.

Message on Chinamen in Cuba. President U. S. Grant. March 20, 1872. H. R. Ex. Docs., No. 207, 42d Cong., 2d sess.

Memorial Relating to Cuba. Citizens of New York City. Dec. 17, 1873. H. R. Misc. Docs., No. 41, 43d Cong., 1st sess.

Message on Capture of the Steamer *Virginius*.

President U. S. Grant. Jan. 5, 1874. H. R. Ex. Docs., No. 30, 43d Cong., 1st sess.

Resolution on Neutrality toward Spain and Cuba. Senator Conover. Jan. 10, 1876. Senate Misc. Docs., No. 29, 44th Cong., 1st sess.

Message Relating to Cuba. President U. S. Grant. Jan. 21, 1876. H. R. Ex. Docs., No. 90, 44th Cong., 1st sess.

Message on the *Virginius* Indemnity. President R. B. Hayes. Nov. 15, 1877. H. R. Ex. Docs., No. 15, 45th Cong., 1st sess.

Message on Seizure of Steamer *Virginius*. President R. B. Hayes. March 29, 1878. H. R. Ex. Docs., No. 72, 45th Cong., 2d sess.

Message on the Insurrection in Cuba. President R. B. Hayes. May 14, 1878. Senate Ex. Docs., No. 79, 45th Cong., 2d sess.

PAGE REFERENCES TO CUBAN REPORTS IN MONTHLY CONSULAR REPORTS FROM MAY, 1893, NO. 152, TO APRIL, 1896, NO. 187.

No.
152, p. 255, Sugar in.
161, p. 346, Iron and manganese ore in.
164, p. 151, Markets for American flour.
165, p. 255, Sugar exports.
167, pp. 630, Tobacco interests; 632, Economic condition.
168, p. 20, Eucalyptus tree.
169, p. 248, Sugar interests.

No.

THE END.

Henry Holt & Co.'s

Newest Books.

International Bimetallism.

By FRANCIS A. WALKER. 3d edition. $1.25.
" In our opinion the best book yet published in the English language for the exposition of the distinctively economic questions at issue between bimetallists and monometallists."—*The Outlook.* "An elaborate study of bimetallism from the first bimetallist in the United States, and there is not a syllable in it that is favorable to the free, unlimited, and independent coinage of silver by the United States."—*Christian Register.* "The silver measure of 1890 Mr. Walker denounces as ' of a thoroughly mischievous character and effect.' So here is the apostle of the bimetallist school in the United States taking the very breath of oratory out of the mouths of Messrs. Bryan, Watson, Bland, Teller, *et al.*"—*N. Y. Commercial Advertiser.*

In India.

By ANDRÉ CHEVRILLON. Translated by William Marchant. 12mo, $1.50.
" No other than a poet with sensibilities quickly responsive to every impression of nature, and the mystery of life dominated by the profoundly impressive religions of the Orient, could have written such a book."—*Book Buyer.*

The Island of Cuba.

By Lieut. A. S. ROWAN, U. S. A., and Prof. M. M. RAMSAY. 12mo.
A clear, compact, impartial, and comprehensive account of the present revolution, and the position of the United States in regard to it, of Cuba's earlier history, her resources, government, religious peculiarities, etc. A bibliography, numerous maps, and a full index are included.

Social Forces in German Literature.

By Prof. KUNO FRANCKE. 8vo, $2.00 *net.*
" A noble contribution to the history of civilization, and valuable not only to students of German literature, but to all who are interested in the progress of our race."—*Hon. Andrew D. White of Cornell.* "It presents the record of German literary achievement from the earliest historical epoch to the end of the nineteenth century in a fresh, sympathetic, and readable form."—*N. Y. Times.*

Henry Holt & Co.'s Newest Books.

Richard Brinsley Sheridan.

A Biography. By W. FRASER RAE. With an Introduction by Sheridan's great-grandson, the Marquess of Dufferin and Ava. With portraits, etc. 2 vols., 8vo, $7.00.

"A story of romantic and human interest."—*Atlantic Monthly.* "A marvelously ingenious and deft piece of biographical narration... Mr. Rae has told a full and interesting story, and has told it well."—*N. Y. Tribune.* "The best biography of Sheridan in existence."—*Review of Reviews.*

On Parody.

By ARTHUR SHADWELL MARTIN. An essay on the art, and humorous selections. 12mo, $1.25.

"Of infinite delight and resource to lovers of English verse."—*The Outlook.* "A very interesting and enjoyable book."—*Boston Transcript.* "Full of good examples."— *The Nation.*

Russian Politics.

By HERBERT M. THOMPSON. With maps. 12mo, $2.00.

"The result of careful study, compactly, clearly, and effectively presented... His work is vivified by the fact that his heart is in it."—*The Outlook.* "One of the best compilations which we have seen for a long time. Nothing abrupt or scrappy about it... Its interest is undeniable."—*The Nation.* "Most intelligible and interesting."—*Atlantic Monthly.*

Animal Symbolism in Ecclesiastical Architecture.

By E. P. EVANS. With a Bibliography and 78 Illustrations. 12mo, buckram, $2.00 *net.*

"Replete with learning, and the fruit of accurate, intelligent observation."—*The Independent.* "Has an immense amount of example and illustration which will be useful to the scholar, while it is a perfect mine of entertainment."—*The Dial.*

Modern Europe.

1792–1878. By C. A. FYFFE. 1 vol., 12mo, $2.75 *net.* 3 vols., 8vo, $7.50.

"As brilliant a sketch as we have seen for many a day."— *The Nation.* "It is by far the most important history published."—*Boston Advertiser.*

Biographical Sketches of the Graduates of Yale College.

With Annals of the College History. By Prof. F. B. DEXTER. 8vo. Vol. I., 1701–45 ; Vol. II., 1745–63. Each, $5.00 *net.*

www.ingramcontent.com/pod-product-compliance
Lightning Source LLC
Chambersburg PA
CBHW020936120726
47905CB00008B/2550